Hope and Recovery
A Chaplain's Handbook

Hope and Recovery - A Chaplain's Handbook

Kayumba David

Published by Kayumba David, 2024.

While every precaution has been taken in the preparation of this book, the publisher assumes no responsibility for errors or omissions, or for damages resulting from the use of the information contained herein.

HOPE AND RECOVERY - A CHAPLAIN'S HANDBOOK

First edition. November 9, 2024.

Copyright © 2024 Kayumba David.

ISBN: 979-8227854780

Written by Kayumba David.

Also by Kayumba David

1
Grow a Backbone and Walk out of an Abusive Marriage

Standalone
Cry Africa The Western Guide on How Not to Fail the Continent
Grow a Backbone and Walk out of an Abusive Marriage
Hope and Healing: A Chaplain's Handbook
REVERSING TYPE 2 DIABETES NATURALLY
Visas: The Irony of Freedom
A Meeting with Majesty: The King's Call to Humanity
Visas: The Irony of Freedom
Love Beyond Time A Comedy of Divine Connection
Silent Complicity: State Sovereignty, Global Inaction, and the
Rwandan Genocide
Bridging the Rift: A Pacifist Vision for the Israel-Palestine Future
Thanks to Calvary: A Salvific Treatise on the Cross
The centuries old swindlers
Harvesting Illusions: The Global Greed and the Pan-African Paradox
Hope and Recovery - A Chaplain's Handbook
The Only Crying God in all the Universe

Watch for more at www.zcews.org.

To all ministers of God News

Kayumba David Kay

Acknowledgments

I would like to express my heartfelt gratitude to my family, whose unwavering support and encouragement have been my foundation throughout this journey. Your love and belief in my calling have inspired me to pursue this vocation with passion and commitment.

I would also like to extend my special thanks to Rachael. Your music possesses an incredible power to bring hope and light to the darkest places. Whether through the soft melodies that soothe a troubled soul or the uplifting rhythms that inspire joy, your talent has been a constant reminder of the healing power of art. Thank you for sharing your gift with the world and for being a source of inspiration in my life.

This book is a reflection of not only my experiences but also the love and encouragement I have received from all of you.

Preface

As a survivor of a challenging illness, I have experienced firsthand the profound impact that compassionate care can have on individuals in their most vulnerable moments. My journey through a robust healthcare environment in Belgium illuminated the critical role that various professionals play in the healing process. Nurses, doctors, and countless other healthcare staff dedicate themselves to the well-being of their patients, often going above and beyond to ensure that each person feels valued and cared for. Their unwavering commitment to service inspires not only hope but also a sense of dignity during difficult times.

In writing this book, I am compelled to reflect on the significant contributions of those who serve in hospitals and other care settings, particularly chaplains who offer spiritual guidance and emotional support. They are the quiet yet powerful voices that provide comfort, instilling hope where despair often threatens to take root. Chaplains walk alongside patients and families, navigating the challenges of illness, suffering, and the uncertainty of life and death.

This guide aims to illuminate the path of chaplaincy in various environments, particularly within hospitals and prisons. It is a call to those who feel the tug of a sacred vocation, encouraging them to embrace their role as vessels of God's love and grace. It is my hope that this book serves as a source of inspiration and practical guidance for current and future chaplains, empowering them to foster healing, reconciliation, and transformation in the lives of those they serve.

May this work resonate with anyone who seeks to understand the beauty and importance of compassionate ministry, reminding us all of the profound difference that care and hope can make in our world.

Table of Contents

Preface

This book, *The Call to Chaplaincy: A Practical Guide to Prison and Hospital Ministry*, is an exploration of the profound and demanding journey that chaplains undertake in service to God's people. Serving in prisons and hospitals, chaplains provide spiritual guidance, comfort, and hope in some of life's most challenging circumstances. This guide seeks to equip chaplains with theological understanding, practical skills, and emotional resilience as they navigate the sacred responsibilities that come with ministering to those on the margins of society.

CHAPTER 1

Introduction to Chaplaincy

Chaplaincy is a serious divine undertaking, for its purpose is to serve not only members of our society but the heirs of God's kingdom. Before we embark on this journey, we must first be sure that the call was issued by the eternal God, and that it is His choice of us, before it becomes our own decision.

Its purpose transcends the basic responsibility of tending to the emotional and social well-being of individuals. As chaplains, we are called to serve not only members of our earthly society but, more significantly, the heirs of God's eternal kingdom. The ministry of chaplaincy demands that we first seek confirmation from the eternal God that this is indeed His calling for us. Before we embark on this journey, we must be certain that the call to chaplaincy is not merely a personal choice but a divine assignment. It must be God's selection of us before it becomes our own decision.

Answering this call requires more than the willingness to fulfill a job description. It involves stepping into a sacred vocation that demands deep spiritual conviction and maturity. The chaplain's role is not simply to offer comfort, guidance, or even spiritual care to individuals at their time of need; it is to serve as a conduit through which God's love, grace, and healing flow. Chaplains must remain mindful that they are working with individuals who, regardless of their physical condition or societal status, have eternal destinies. Our work is not only to address the temporary and physical concerns of the moment but to tend to the soul, the immortal part of each person we encounter.

The Nature of the Call to Chaplaincy

Chaplaincy is not for the faint of heart. It demands a heart of compassion, an unwavering faith, and a willingness to minister in some of the most emotionally and spiritually demanding environments. Whether in hospitals, where sickness, suffering, and the proximity of death are constant companions, or in prisons, where brokenness, isolation, and alienation dominate the lives of inmates, chaplains are called to walk alongside individuals at their lowest points.

This calling requires a unique combination of spiritual, emotional, and psychological fortitude. Chaplains are often called to bear witness to human suffering in its most raw and unfiltered form. The environments in which chaplains serve can be deeply unsettling—places where pain, despair, and hopelessness often overshadow hope and healing. Yet, the chaplain is sent into these dark spaces with a divine mission: to bring light, hope, and healing to those in need.

The presence of a chaplain in these challenging environments is not coincidental; it is intentional. Chaplains act as beacons of God's love and compassion, helping to carry the burdens of those who suffer and guiding them toward spiritual peace and reconciliation. For those in hospitals, chaplains offer a comforting presence, helping patients and families cope with illness, trauma, and the uncertainties surrounding life and death. For those in prisons, chaplains offer inmates the opportunity for redemption, forgiveness, and healing—a chance to reconcile their past and seek a transformed future.

Chaplaincy as a Ministry of Presence

One of the most profound aspects of chaplaincy is the ministry of presence. The chaplain's role is not always to offer answers, solve problems, or even provide religious instruction. Sometimes, the most significant gift a chaplain can give is simply being present. This ministry of presence embodies the love and compassion of God by offering a non-judgmental, listening ear and a compassionate heart.

In hospitals, patients may be grappling with their mortality, wrestling with questions of faith, or feeling isolated in their suffering. Family members may be struggling to make difficult decisions about medical treatment, or they may be grieving the impending loss of a loved one. In these moments of vulnerability, the chaplain's presence brings comfort, hope, and spiritual care that acknowledges the sacredness of human life and the significance of eternal matters.

In prisons, inmates often feel abandoned by society and separated from their families and communities. They may be wrestling with guilt, shame, and a sense of hopelessness about their future. The chaplain's ministry of presence provides a glimmer of hope—a reminder that even in the darkest of places, God's grace can penetrate, heal, and transform. By simply showing up, sitting with an inmate, listening to their story, and offering a word of encouragement, the chaplain reflects the unconditional love of God, who never abandons His children, no matter how far they may have fallen.

The Chaplain's Role: A Bridge Between Faith, Hope, and Healing

Chaplains occupy a unique position as they serve as bridges between the physical world and the spiritual realm. In hospitals, they are part of the healthcare team, offering spiritual care alongside medical treatment. In prisons, they provide spiritual support amidst a system focused on punishment and rehabilitation. Yet, the chaplain's role extends beyond the boundaries of these institutions; they are called to bridge the gap between despair and hope, brokenness and healing, guilt and forgiveness.

As a bridge, the chaplain facilitates the process of healing in a holistic manner. Healing, in the biblical sense, is not just physical restoration, but the restoration of the whole person—mind, body, and soul. Chaplains are equipped to offer spiritual care that addresses the inner wounds of the individuals they serve. They help those in their care find meaning in their suffering, discover the grace of forgiveness, and receive the hope of eternal life. Whether through prayer, spiritual counseling, or simply being a compassionate presence, chaplains lead people toward the One who offers ultimate healing—Jesus Christ.

The Biblical and Theological Foundations of Chaplaincy

The work of chaplaincy is firmly rooted in the biblical call to serve "the least of these" (Matthew 25:40). Jesus' ministry on earth consistently demonstrated a deep care for those who were marginalized, suffering, or in need of healing. He ministered to the sick, comforted the grieving, and offered forgiveness to sinners. This example is the foundation of chaplaincy. Chaplains are called to continue this ministry of compassionate care, following in the footsteps of Christ, who came "not to be served, but to serve" (Mark 10:45).

Chaplains embody the love of God in practical ways, serving as the hands and feet of Christ in a world where suffering and injustice still exist. They provide spiritual care that reflects the heart of God, who desires that none should perish but that all should come to repentance (2 Peter 3:9). This ministry is not limited to any particular religious denomination or community; chaplains serve all people, regardless of their faith, background, or beliefs, recognizing the inherent dignity of every person as made in the image of God.

The Cost of Chaplaincy: Sacrifice and Spiritual Growth

Serving as a chaplain comes with personal cost. Chaplains often deal with emotional and spiritual exhaustion as they consistently give of themselves to those who are hurting. The burden of witnessing pain, grief, and death on a regular basis can take its toll on even the most spiritually mature individuals. This is why chaplains must prioritize their own spiritual health and well-being. Regular prayer, reflection, and connection with God are essential to maintaining the strength and resilience needed for ministry.

Chaplains are called to walk the difficult path of self-sacrifice, pouring out their lives for the sake of others, just as Christ poured out His life for us. This selfless service requires not only a deep faith but also a willingness to be transformed by the very work they do. Chaplaincy is not just about ministering to others; it is a journey of spiritual growth for the chaplain as well. Through the trials, challenges, and rewards of ministry, chaplains are refined and drawn closer to God.

Conclusion

Chaplaincy is a divine calling, one that requires deep spiritual conviction, emotional resilience, and a heart committed to serving God's people in their most vulnerable moments. It is a ministry of presence, hope, and healing, rooted in the biblical mandate to care for the least of these. Chaplains are called to be the hands and feet of Christ, bringing light to dark places and offering spiritual care that addresses the whole person—body, mind, and spirit. For those who are called to this sacred work, chaplaincy is both a profound privilege and a humbling responsibility. May those who answer this call do so with courage, compassion, and a heart surrendered to the will of God.

Chapter 2: Preparing for Ministry

Developing the Pastoral Heart: Empathy, Patience, and Presence

Being a chaplain is more than performing duties or fulfilling a job description; it is about embodying the love of God through the pastoral heart. A chaplain's ministry centers on the ability to listen deeply, be patient in difficult moments, and remain present as a source of strength and comfort. Developing the pastoral heart involves cultivating the qualities of empathy, patience, and presence—qualities that are essential in providing spiritual and emotional care to those in need. These traits are not simply skills to be learned, but virtues to be nurtured through prayer, reflection, and active ministry. Let's explore how chaplains can grow in these qualities and integrate them into their daily ministry.

Empathy: The Heart of Pastoral Care

Empathy is the cornerstone of chaplaincy. At its core, empathy is the ability to understand and share the feelings of another. In chaplaincy, this means being able to step into the shoes of those you are serving, seeing the world through their eyes, and feeling their pain, joy, fear, or grief as your own. It goes beyond sympathy, which involves feeling for someone, to genuinely feeling with someone.

For chaplains, empathy is essential because they often minister to people in moments of profound vulnerability—whether it's a patient receiving a terminal diagnosis, a family grieving a loved one, or an inmate grappling with guilt and shame. In these moments, people are looking for more than words of comfort; they are looking for someone who truly understands, someone who will sit with them in their pain without trying to fix it or make it go away.

Practicing Empathy: Listening Without Judgment

One of the most powerful ways chaplains can show empathy is by practicing deep, non-judgmental listening. Too often, people feel unheard or dismissed, especially in settings like hospitals and prisons, where they may feel depersonalized by systems and procedures. A chaplain who listens carefully, without interrupting, offering solutions, or making judgments, gives the person they are serving the gift of being truly seen and heard.

Empathy requires that chaplains set aside their own agendas, biases, and preconceptions in order to fully engage with the person in front of them. This may mean listening to stories of deep regret, anger, or fear—emotions that can make us uncomfortable. Yet, by being present with these emotions without trying to change them, chaplains demonstrate a Christ-like compassion that allows others to feel safe in sharing their pain.

To foster empathy, chaplains must cultivate a habit of prayer and reflection. Through prayer, chaplains can seek God's guidance to soften their hearts, open their minds, and enable them to love others as Christ loves them. Reflecting on one's own experiences of pain and vulnerability can also help chaplains develop a deeper understanding of the human condition and the importance of being present with others in their suffering.

Patience: Enduring with Grace

Patience is another key element of the pastoral heart. In the context of chaplaincy, patience involves more than simply waiting for a situation to change; it is about enduring adversity with grace, both in your own life and in the lives of those you serve. Chaplains often work in environments where change is slow, where people may not be ready to confront their pain, and where healing—spiritually, emotionally, or physically—may take time. In these settings, patience becomes a vital quality.

For example, in a hospital, a patient may be struggling with their faith, questioning God's presence in their suffering, or feeling anger and despair. The chaplain's role is not to push for a resolution or quick spiritual answers, but to be patient, offering gentle support and guidance as the patient works through these difficult emotions. Similarly, in a prison setting, an inmate may resist spiritual transformation or reconciliation. The chaplain must patiently walk with them, trusting that God is at work, even when the results are not immediately visible.

The Practice of Patience in Ministry

Patience in chaplaincy is about trusting God's timing. Chaplains must resist the urge to force outcomes, remembering that spiritual and emotional growth often occur in ways we cannot control or predict. Instead of focusing on quick fixes or immediate changes, chaplains are called to nurture long-term healing and transformation.

To develop patience, chaplains need to practice the spiritual discipline of waiting on God. This involves surrendering our desire for control and trusting that God is present and active, even in situations that seem stagnant or unresolved. Regular prayer and meditation can help chaplains cultivate a patient spirit, as they learn to rely on God's strength rather than their own. Reflection on the patience of Christ, who bore with His disciples' misunderstandings and failures with grace, can inspire chaplains to extend the same patience to those they serve.

Presence: The Ministry of Being

Perhaps the most unique aspect of chaplaincy is the ministry of presence. In a world that often values action, solutions, and productivity, chaplains offer something different: the gift of simply being present. The ministry of presence is about showing up—not to fix, solve, or explain, but to stand alongside someone in their suffering, offering your undivided attention and compassionate presence.

In both hospitals and prisons, chaplains are often faced with situations where there are no easy answers, no solutions that can alleviate the suffering of those they serve. In these moments, the chaplain's presence itself becomes a form of ministry. Being present with someone in their pain, without trying to change their experience or take away their discomfort, can offer deep comfort and healing.

The ministry of presence reflects the incarnational nature of God's love. Just as God, in the person of Jesus, entered into our world and walked alongside us in our humanity, chaplains are called to enter into the lives of those they serve, bearing witness to their struggles and offering a compassionate, non-judgmental presence. By being fully present with others, chaplains provide a tangible reminder that God is with us, even in our darkest moments.

Practicing the Ministry of Presence

The ministry of presence requires a chaplain to be fully engaged, both mentally and emotionally, in the moment. This means putting aside distractions, worries, and even the temptation to offer advice, in order to be fully attuned to the person in front of you. It involves creating a space of peace and safety where people feel free to express their emotions, knowing they will be met with compassion and understanding.

Developing this quality requires intentional practice. Chaplains must cultivate mindfulness and attentiveness, learning to focus on the present moment and the needs of the individual they are serving. Prayer and contemplation are crucial in this process, as they allow chaplains to center themselves in God's presence before entering into the ministry of presence with others.

Moreover, chaplains should reflect on how Christ was present with people during His earthly ministry. Jesus did not rush through His encounters with others, nor did He offer quick fixes to their problems. Instead, He was fully present, taking time to listen, understand, and show compassion. By following His example, chaplains can embody this same ministry of presence, offering others a glimpse of God's unconditional love and care.

Conclusion: Nurturing the Pastoral Heart

The pastoral heart is one that listens with empathy, endures with patience, and remains fully present with those who are suffering. These qualities are essential for chaplains, who are called to serve people in some of the most challenging moments of their lives. Developing the pastoral heart is a lifelong process that requires ongoing prayer, reflection, and intentional practice.

Chaplains must continually seek God's help in cultivating empathy, patience, and presence, knowing that these virtues do not come naturally but are the fruit of a deep and abiding relationship with God. By nurturing the pastoral heart, chaplains can offer a ministry that reflects the heart of Christ—one that is compassionate, patient, and present, even in the midst of suffering.

As chaplains grow in these qualities, they become instruments of God's healing and grace, bringing comfort to those who are hurting and reminding them that they are not alone in their journey. The pastoral heart, rooted in the love of God, enables chaplains to fulfill their sacred calling with compassion, courage, and faith.

Essential Spiritual Disciplines for Chaplains

Chaplains are constantly on the front lines of human suffering, encountering people at their most vulnerable. Whether in hospitals, prisons, or other settings, chaplains witness pain, grief, loss, and despair daily. To serve effectively in these challenging environments, chaplains must remain spiritually grounded and resilient. This requires intentional engagement in spiritual disciplines that provide nourishment for the soul, strength for the body, and clarity for the mind.

Spiritual disciplines such as prayer, study, reflection, and care are essential tools for chaplains, helping them stay connected to God, maintain emotional balance, and deepen their pastoral effectiveness. These practices not only sustain the chaplain's own spiritual life but also enable them to minister more compassionately and effectively to others. Let's explore each of these spiritual disciplines and how they contribute to the chaplain's overall well-being and ministry.

Prayer: The Foundation of Chaplaincy

Prayer is the most fundamental spiritual discipline for any chaplain. It is the primary way that chaplains communicate with God, seeking His guidance, strength, and wisdom as they serve others. Prayer nurtures the chaplain's relationship with God and keeps them rooted in their calling. Without a consistent and deep prayer life, chaplains risk losing their spiritual vitality and becoming disconnected from the source of their ministry—God Himself.

For chaplains, prayer takes many forms. It can be intercessory prayer, where they lift up the needs of the people they serve—praying for healing, comfort, forgiveness, or strength. It can also be contemplative prayer, where chaplains sit quietly in God's presence, listening for His voice and allowing His peace to fill their hearts. In moments of exhaustion or uncertainty, prayer can also be a time of surrender, where chaplains bring their burdens before God, trusting Him to carry them.

In the busy and emotionally charged environment of chaplaincy, prayer acts as a lifeline. It is the chaplain's way of staying connected to the source of all comfort and strength, ensuring that they do not rely solely on their own abilities but lean on God's grace. Regular, intentional prayer helps chaplains maintain a posture of humility and dependence on God, which is essential for their own spiritual health and the effectiveness of their ministry.

Study: Deepening Understanding and Wisdom

In addition to prayer, regular study of Scripture and other theological resources is essential for chaplains. Theological study equips chaplains with a deeper understanding of their faith, giving them the wisdom and insight needed to provide spiritual care in complex situations. Whether navigating ethical dilemmas in a hospital or addressing issues of guilt and forgiveness in a prison, chaplains must have a strong grasp of biblical principles and theological truths.

Studying Scripture allows chaplains to grow in their knowledge of God's Word and discern His will for their ministry. It provides a foundation for preaching, teaching, and counseling, ensuring that the chaplain's words and actions are rooted in biblical truth. Scripture study also helps chaplains cultivate a spirit of discernment, enabling them to minister with sensitivity and wisdom in diverse and challenging contexts.

In addition to Scripture, chaplains should engage with other theological, pastoral, and psychological resources. Reading books on pastoral care, ethics, and spiritual counseling can provide valuable insights and practical tools for chaplaincy work. Likewise, engaging with works of Christian spirituality—both ancient and modern—can deepen the chaplain's understanding of prayer, suffering, and the human experience. Ongoing study helps chaplains stay intellectually engaged and spiritually nourished, ensuring they continue to grow in their ministry.

Reflection: Self-Awareness and Growth

Reflection is a critical spiritual discipline for chaplains, offering a space to process their experiences, emotions, and spiritual growth. Chaplains are constantly encountering people in difficult circumstances, and these encounters can leave a lasting emotional and spiritual impact. Without intentional reflection, chaplains risk becoming overwhelmed by the weight of the suffering they witness.

Reflection provides chaplains with the opportunity to step back from the busyness of their ministry and consider how God is at work in their lives and the lives of those they serve. It allows them to process difficult encounters, ask questions about their own responses, and discern where they need to grow in compassion, patience, or understanding. Reflection also helps chaplains stay aware of their own emotional and spiritual needs, ensuring that they take time for self-care and avoid burnout.

There are many ways chaplains can engage in reflection. Journaling is one powerful tool for self-reflection, allowing chaplains to write down their thoughts, prayers, and experiences. This practice not only helps chaplains process their emotions but also provides a record of God's faithfulness and guidance throughout their ministry. Regular retreats, spiritual direction, or conversations with a mentor or fellow chaplain can also be valuable opportunities for reflection and growth.

By engaging in reflection, chaplains develop greater self-awareness, which helps them minister more effectively to others. They become more attuned to their own strengths and weaknesses, allowing them to approach their ministry with humility and openness to God's continued work in their lives.

Care: Nurturing the Body, Mind, and Soul

While prayer, study, and reflection nourish the chaplain's spiritual life, the discipline of care focuses on the holistic well-being of the chaplain. Ministry can be physically, emotionally, and mentally exhausting, and chaplains must take intentional steps to care for their own health in order to serve others effectively. Self-care is not a selfish act; it is a vital part of being a sustainable and effective chaplain.

Caring for the body means making time for rest, exercise, and proper nutrition. Chaplains often work long hours in emotionally intense environments, and neglecting physical health can lead to burnout or illness. Maintaining physical well-being ensures that chaplains have the energy and resilience to continue their demanding work.

Mental and emotional care is equally important. Chaplains frequently encounter difficult and traumatic situations, which can take a toll on their emotional health. Seeking regular support—whether through counseling, peer groups, or spiritual direction—can help chaplains process their experiences and prevent emotional fatigue. Engaging in hobbies, spending time with loved ones, and taking breaks from ministry are also essential components of emotional care.

Finally, soul care involves nurturing one's relationship with God. This is done through spiritual disciplines like prayer and reflection but also through practices that bring joy and refreshment. Chaplains may find renewal in nature, worship, art, or other activities that allow them to experience God's presence in new and meaningful ways. By caring for their own spiritual well-being, chaplains ensure that they are ministering from a place of fullness, rather than depletion.

The Integration of Spiritual Disciplines

Spiritual disciplines are not isolated practices; they are deeply interconnected and work together to strengthen the chaplain's ministry. Prayer nurtures the chaplain's relationship with God, while study deepens their understanding of His Word. Reflection helps chaplains process their experiences and grow in self-awareness, while care ensures that they remain healthy and resilient in body, mind, and soul. Together, these disciplines create a strong foundation for chaplaincy work, enabling chaplains to serve others effectively while nurturing their own spiritual well-being.

The life of a chaplain is a life of service, but it must also be a life of spiritual discipline. By intentionally engaging in practices that foster spiritual growth, chaplains ensure that they remain connected to God, grounded in their calling, and equipped to face the challenges of ministry with grace and resilience.

Conclusion

Essential spiritual disciplines such as prayer, study, reflection, and care are the lifeblood of a chaplain's ministry. These practices provide the spiritual nourishment and emotional resilience needed to minister effectively to others, even in the most challenging circumstances. By cultivating a regular discipline of prayer, engaging in deep theological study, reflecting on their experiences, and taking care of their own physical, emotional, and spiritual health, chaplains are better equipped to embody God's love and compassion in their ministry.

In the end, chaplaincy is a deeply spiritual vocation, one that requires not only a heart for others but also a heart for God. Through the consistent practice of spiritual disciplines, chaplains ensure that they remain rooted in their calling and connected to the One who sustains them. By nurturing their own souls, they become better instruments of God's grace, offering hope, healing, and love to those they are called to serve.

Basic Counseling Skills and Active Listening

Chaplains frequently serve as informal counselors to individuals going through crises, trauma, and profound emotional or spiritual struggles. Whether in a hospital, prison, or other settings, people often turn to chaplains for guidance, comfort, and support in some of the darkest moments of their lives. As a result, chaplains need to develop essential counseling skills that will allow them to provide meaningful, non-judgmental support and be a compassionate presence to those in need.

The role of the chaplain is not necessarily that of a trained therapist, but rather one of spiritual and emotional care. By mastering skills such as active listening, asking thoughtful questions, and providing supportive, judgment-free guidance, chaplains can offer the help that people need in times of distress. This section will explore these fundamental counseling skills, emphasizing the value of being fully present and engaged in each interaction.

Active Listening: The Foundation of Chaplaincy

Active listening is the bedrock of effective counseling and one of the most important skills a chaplain can cultivate. In any pastoral encounter, especially with people in crisis, the first and most important task is to listen. Listening, however, is more than simply hearing someone's words—it involves fully engaging with the person, paying attention to their emotions, body language, and the deeper meaning behind what they are saying.

Active listening requires the chaplain to be fully present, setting aside their own thoughts, judgments, and agendas in order to focus entirely on the person in front of them. It is a form of ministry in itself, as it communicates to the person that they are valued, heard, and understood. In an environment where people may often feel overlooked or dismissed, the gift of truly listening can be incredibly healing.

Some key elements of active listening include:

- **Non-verbal cues**: Maintaining eye contact, nodding, and using body language to show that you are engaged. These non-verbal signals communicate that you are attentive and present in the conversation.

- **Reflecting emotions**: Paying attention to the emotions the person is expressing and reflecting them back. For example, if someone is describing a painful experience, a chaplain might say, "It sounds like you're feeling overwhelmed right now." This helps the person feel understood and validated.

- **Avoiding interruptions**: Allowing the person to speak without interrupting or rushing to offer advice. This shows respect for their experience and gives them space to fully express themselves.

- **Summarizing and clarifying**: Periodically summarizing what the person has said to ensure that you have understood correctly. This might sound like, "So, what I'm hearing is that you're feeling confused about what to do next." Clarifying helps avoid misunderstandings and confirms that you are truly listening.

Through active listening, chaplains not only gather important information about the person's emotional and spiritual state, but they also create a safe space for the individual to process their thoughts and feelings. This simple but powerful skill is often more valuable than any words of advice or guidance.

Asking the Right Questions: Guiding Conversations with Sensitivity

While active listening is foundational, chaplains must also know how to ask the right questions in order to guide the conversation in a helpful direction. The questions a chaplain asks can help individuals gain clarity about their situation, explore their emotions, and discover their own inner resources for healing. However, it is important that these questions be open-ended and non-directive, allowing the person to lead the conversation in a way that feels comfortable for them.

Open-ended questions are especially valuable in chaplaincy because they invite the person to share more deeply, rather than simply responding with "yes" or "no." These types of questions encourage reflection and self-exploration. Examples of open-ended questions might include:

- "Can you tell me more about what's been happening lately?"
- "How are you feeling about what's going on?"
- "What has been the hardest part of this experience for you?"
- "Where do you see God in this situation?"

The goal of these questions is not to direct the person toward a particular conclusion, but to allow them the freedom to express their thoughts and feelings. Chaplains must resist the urge to ask **leading questions** that impose a particular point of view, such as, "Don't you think things will get better soon?" or "Have you tried praying about it?" These types of questions can feel dismissive or judgmental and may shut down the person's openness to share.

Instead, chaplains should aim to ask questions that help the person explore their own experience, emotions, and spiritual journey. **Follow-up questions** can also be helpful in encouraging deeper reflection. For example, after someone shares a difficult emotion, a chaplain might ask, "What do you think is behind that feeling?" or "How has this experience affected your faith?"

By asking thoughtful, open-ended questions, chaplains help individuals gain insight into their situation, which can lead to healing and spiritual growth. The key is to approach these conversations with curiosity, compassion, and a genuine desire to understand.

Offering Non-Judgmental Support: Creating a Safe Space for Healing

One of the greatest gifts a chaplain can offer is non-judgmental support. People in crisis often feel vulnerable, ashamed, or afraid of being judged for their feelings, choices, or circumstances. Chaplains must create a space where individuals feel safe to express themselves without fear of criticism or condemnation.

Non-judgmental support means accepting the person where they are, without trying to change them or fix their problems. This doesn't mean that chaplains endorse every behavior or decision, but rather that they recognize the person's inherent dignity and worth, regardless of their struggles. In a prison setting, for example, an inmate may feel unworthy of God's love due to past mistakes. The chaplain's role is not to judge their past but to offer compassion, understanding, and a reminder of God's grace and forgiveness.

Some ways chaplains can offer non-judgmental support include:

- **Validating emotions**: Letting people know that it's okay to feel what they are feeling, whether that's anger, sadness, confusion, or fear. Statements like "It's understandable that you feel this way" can help individuals feel seen and heard.
- **Avoiding advice-giving**: Rather than immediately offering solutions or advice, chaplains should focus on listening and empathizing. Advice-giving can sometimes feel dismissive, as it implies that the person's feelings

or experiences are easily solved with a quick fix.

- **Holding space for silence**: Sometimes, the best way to support someone is simply to sit with them in silence. Chaplains don't need to fill every moment with words—silence can be a powerful way to honor the person's experience and allow them time to reflect.

- **Offering hope without false reassurances**: It's important for chaplains to offer hope in the face of despair, but this must be done with sensitivity. Rather than making unrealistic promises ("Everything will work out"), chaplains can offer a more grounded hope rooted in faith and God's presence, such as, "I believe God is with you, even in this difficult time."

Non-judgmental support is about being with people in their pain, offering them unconditional care, and trusting that God is at work in their lives, even if the path to healing is not immediately clear.

Conclusion: Combining Counseling Skills for Effective Ministry

Basic counseling skills such as active listening, asking thoughtful questions, and offering non-judgmental support are crucial tools in the chaplain's ministry. These skills allow chaplains to provide compassionate care that respects the dignity and autonomy of the individuals they serve. By listening deeply, guiding conversations with sensitivity, and offering unconditional support, chaplains create a space where healing, growth, and spiritual transformation can occur.

These skills are not just about providing emotional support—they are an extension of the chaplain's pastoral calling to embody the love and compassion of Christ. Through careful attention to the needs of others and a commitment to being fully present in each interaction, chaplains serve as vessels of God's grace in some of the most challenging and painful moments of life. In doing so, they fulfill their sacred calling to offer light in places of darkness and hope in moments of despair.

Navigating Interfaith Ministry

Chaplains often serve in environments that bring them into contact with people from a wide range of religious and spiritual traditions. Hospitals, prisons, military settings, and other institutions are increasingly diverse, both culturally and religiously. As a result, one of the most important skills a chaplain must develop is the ability to navigate interfaith ministry with sensitivity and respect.

Interfaith ministry does not require a chaplain to abandon or compromise their own faith, but it does require an understanding of and respect for the beliefs and practices of others. Chaplains serve people at vulnerable points in their lives—times of sickness, death, incarceration, or crisis—and in these moments, individuals often seek comfort and guidance from their spiritual beliefs. To be effective in ministry, chaplains must be prepared to meet people where they are spiritually, even when their faith traditions differ from their own.

This section explores the challenges and opportunities of interfaith ministry and provides practical guidance on how to minister effectively in a diverse spiritual landscape.

The Importance of Religious Sensitivity

In interfaith settings, religious sensitivity is paramount. Chaplains must be aware that the people they serve come from a variety of backgrounds, each with its own set of beliefs, rituals, and expectations. Ignorance of or disregard for these differences can alienate those seeking spiritual care and may even cause harm.

For example, some religious groups have specific rituals surrounding illness, death, and mourning that are deeply important to them. A chaplain who fails to recognize these traditions might inadvertently disrespect someone's deeply held beliefs. Conversely, a chaplain who demonstrates understanding and respect for a person's religious practices can build trust and offer meaningful support.

Religious sensitivity begins with **education**. Chaplains should take the time to learn about the major world religions and the spiritual practices they are likely to encounter in their work. This includes understanding the beliefs, rituals, and holidays of various faith traditions, as well as being aware of key differences within those traditions. For example, Christianity itself is diverse, with denominations like Catholicism, Protestantism, and Orthodoxy holding distinct practices and theological understandings. Similarly, Islam has Sunni and Shia branches, and Buddhism has Theravada and Mahayana traditions.

In addition to general knowledge, chaplains should seek to understand the **individual's personal expression** of their faith. Even within a particular religion, people may practice their faith in unique ways. Being open to learning from the individual themselves about what their faith means to them and how they would like to engage with it during a difficult time is an important part of religious sensitivity.

Listening to Understand: The Chaplain as a Learner

In interfaith ministry, the chaplain's primary posture should be one of **listening to understand** rather than assuming expertise or authority over another person's spiritual experience. People may turn to the chaplain for comfort, prayer, or guidance, but they do not expect the chaplain to be an expert in their specific religious tradition. Instead, they often seek someone who will listen compassionately, acknowledge their beliefs, and offer support in alignment with their spiritual needs.

In these situations, **active listening** becomes particularly important. When serving someone from a different faith tradition, chaplains should:

- **Ask open-ended questions** to explore the person's spiritual or religious needs, such as, "How does your faith bring you comfort in this moment?" or "Are there any rituals or prayers that would help you feel supported right now?"
- **Listen without judgment** to what the person says about their beliefs and practices, even if they differ significantly from the chaplain's own faith.
- **Offer validation** by acknowledging the importance of the person's faith in their experience, for instance, "It sounds like your faith is really important to you during this time, and I want to respect that as we move forward."

Through these practices, the chaplain communicates a desire to understand the person's spiritual world and offers support that respects their beliefs.

Ministering Without Compromising Your Own Faith

While interfaith ministry requires openness and respect, it does not demand that chaplains compromise their own beliefs or engage in religious practices that conflict with their faith. For instance, a Christian chaplain may be asked to offer spiritual support to a Muslim patient. The chaplain can be present, offer care, and listen to the patient's spiritual needs without leading them in Islamic prayers if that conflicts with the chaplain's faith tradition.

Instead of participating in specific religious rituals that might conflict with their beliefs, chaplains can offer **non-religious forms of support** that still meet the person's spiritual needs. For example, a chaplain might offer words of comfort, reflect on themes of hope, or simply provide a compassionate presence during a difficult time. Sometimes, just being there as a caring and respectful companion is enough.

It is important for chaplains to recognize their **own boundaries** and to communicate them with humility and grace. If a person requests something outside of the chaplain's faith tradition—such as leading a ritual in a language or manner that is unfamiliar—the chaplain can respectfully decline while still offering support in other ways. They might say, "I'm not familiar with that practice, but I'm happy to sit with you during this time," or, "I'm not able to lead that prayer, but I can find someone from your faith community who can."

In many cases, interfaith ministry also involves **referrals**. Chaplains should build connections with leaders from various faith communities who can provide more specific religious care when needed. For example, if a Jewish patient requests a rabbi for a particular ritual, the chaplain can facilitate that connection, ensuring the patient receives the spiritual care they need from someone who shares their faith.

Being Present Across Religious Divides

In interfaith ministry, the role of the chaplain is often less about **providing specific religious instruction** and more about being a compassionate and attentive presence. Chaplains are called to offer spiritual care across religious divides, and this means being fully present with people in their moment of need, regardless of their faith background.

One of the most powerful ways to do this is through the ministry of **presence**. Often, people in crisis do not need theological answers or religious rituals—they need someone to be with them, to listen, to share in their pain, and to provide a non-anxious presence. This is especially true when serving people from different faith traditions, as the chaplain's simple act of being there can transcend religious differences and speak to the universal human need for connection and support.

For instance, a chaplain may be asked to sit with a family during a loved one's final moments, even though the family practices a different faith. In such a situation, the chaplain doesn't need to offer prayers or religious words specific to that tradition; their quiet presence, empathetic listening, and gentle support can be deeply comforting. This is where the chaplain's role as a **spiritual companion** shines, helping people navigate grief, uncertainty, and pain, regardless of their religious beliefs.

Practical Tips for Navigating Interfaith Ministry

Navigating interfaith ministry can be challenging, but there are practical steps chaplains can take to ensure they approach each situation with respect, understanding, and care:

1. **Educate Yourself**: Take time to learn about the major world religions you are likely to encounter. Understand basic beliefs, rituals, and holidays so that you can engage with people's spiritual needs knowledgeably.

2. **Ask Respectful Questions**: If you are unsure about a person's faith or religious practices, ask them respectfully. Allow them to be the expert on their own beliefs and preferences.

3. **Acknowledge Your Limitations**: Be honest about the limits of your own faith knowledge. It's okay to admit that you are unfamiliar with a particular tradition and to ask for guidance or make a referral.

4. **Cultivate Partnerships**: Build relationships with local religious leaders from a variety of faith communities. This allows you to make referrals when someone needs specific religious care that is outside your expertise.

5. **Stay True to Your Faith**: While it's important to be open and respectful of other traditions, don't feel pressured to compromise your own beliefs or engage in practices that are inconsistent with your faith.

6. **Focus on Universal Values**: Regardless of religious

differences, focus on universal themes like compassion, love, hope, and presence. These are values that transcend specific religious beliefs and can offer deep comfort to people in crisis.

Conclusion: The Chaplain as a Bridge

In today's diverse and pluralistic world, chaplains serve as bridges between people of different faiths and beliefs. Interfaith ministry is not about diluting one's own faith or becoming an expert in every religious tradition, but about offering compassionate, respectful, and meaningful care to everyone, regardless of their spiritual background. By listening deeply, respecting differences, and remaining true to their own faith, chaplains can navigate interfaith contexts with grace, providing much-needed support in times of need.

Ultimately, interfaith ministry allows chaplains to reflect God's love in a way that speaks to the universal human experience of seeking meaning, comfort, and connection in life's most challenging moments.

Chapter 3: Prison Chaplaincy

The Spiritual and Psychological Needs of Inmates

Incarceration is not just a physical separation from society—it often represents a profound emotional, psychological, and spiritual upheaval for those who experience it. Being imprisoned can strip individuals of their sense of identity, dignity, and purpose, leaving them vulnerable to deep emotional pain and spiritual crises. The isolation, loss of freedom, and social stigma associated with imprisonment can lead inmates to wrestle with feelings of guilt, shame, anger, fear, and hopelessness.

For many inmates, the struggle is twofold: they must navigate both the immediate realities of incarceration—harsh environments, rigid routines, and limited autonomy—while also confronting the long-standing issues that may have contributed to their imprisonment, such as broken relationships, unresolved trauma, and moral failure. As they grapple with these inner and outer struggles, their spiritual and psychological needs become acute, and chaplains have a critical role in meeting those needs.

This section explores the spiritual and psychological crises that inmates commonly face and outlines how chaplains can offer support, guidance, and hope in the midst of incarceration.

Guilt, Shame, and Forgiveness

One of the most common spiritual and psychological struggles inmates face is a deep sense of **guilt** and **shame** over the actions that led to their imprisonment. Many inmates are haunted by their past decisions—whether they involve crime, violence, addiction, or betrayal of loved ones. They may feel that their mistakes define them, locking them into a cycle of self-condemnation and despair.

For some, guilt can serve as a catalyst for spiritual growth. Inmates may seek forgiveness—from God, from the people they've wronged, and from themselves—as a path toward healing and redemption. However, for others, guilt can be paralyzing, driving them into a spiral of self-loathing and hopelessness. This is where the role of the chaplain becomes essential.

Chaplains can help inmates navigate these feelings of guilt by offering a **non-judgmental space** where they can openly reflect on their past actions. Through **pastoral counseling**, chaplains can encourage inmates to acknowledge their wrongdoings while also guiding them toward a process of self-forgiveness and spiritual reconciliation. A key part of this journey is helping inmates understand that while they are responsible for their actions, they are not beyond the reach of **divine grace** and transformation. Whether through scriptural study, prayer, or one-on-one spiritual guidance, chaplains can offer the message that no one is beyond the possibility of **forgiveness** and **redemption**.

In faith traditions like Christianity, the themes of repentance, forgiveness, and grace are particularly significant. Chaplains can guide inmates in seeking God's forgiveness and help them understand that despite their past, they can still experience the love, mercy, and grace of God. For some inmates, this journey toward forgiveness may be the first step in rebuilding their sense of self-worth and hope for the future.

Hopelessness and Finding Meaning

Inmates often experience overwhelming feelings of **hopelessness**, particularly those serving long sentences or facing uncertain futures. The harsh realities of prison life—limited contact with loved ones, lack of freedom, and the dehumanizing nature of incarceration—can strip individuals of their sense of purpose and lead to spiritual despair.

Chaplains can offer inmates a sense of **hope** by helping them find meaning even within the confines of their circumstances. This may involve guiding them in discovering or deepening their faith, cultivating spiritual disciplines like prayer and meditation, or helping them identify ways they can positively impact the prison community.

One way chaplains can foster hope is by encouraging inmates to see their time in prison as an opportunity for **personal transformation**. While they cannot change their past or control their immediate environment, they can choose how they respond to their situation. By engaging in spiritual reflection, self-examination, and the pursuit of positive goals—whether through education, creative expression, or service to others—many inmates can begin to find purpose even behind bars. Chaplains can play a pivotal role in supporting this process by offering spiritual resources, guiding discussions about meaning and purpose, and providing opportunities for spiritual growth.

In addition to individual spiritual support, chaplains can create a sense of hope through **group ministry**, such as leading Bible studies, prayer groups, or spiritual discussion circles. These gatherings not only offer inmates a chance to explore their faith, but also provide a supportive community where they can encourage one another in their spiritual journeys.

Anger, Fear, and Emotional Resilience

Prison can be a place of intense **anger** and **fear**, both of which can undermine an inmate's spiritual and psychological well-being. Some inmates carry deep-seated anger over the circumstances that led to their imprisonment—whether they feel betrayed by society, the justice system, or even their own family members. Others may be consumed by fear, worrying about their safety in the hostile prison environment or about what awaits them upon their release.

Left unchecked, these emotions can lead to destructive behaviors such as aggression, isolation, or hopelessness. Chaplains, however, can offer inmates tools for managing their emotions through spiritual and psychological resilience.

Through **active listening**, chaplains can provide inmates with a safe space to express their anger, fear, and frustration without judgment. This simple act of listening can be incredibly therapeutic for inmates who feel voiceless or ignored. In addition to listening, chaplains can offer **pastoral counseling** that encourages inmates to work through their anger in healthy ways—whether by engaging in prayer, reflecting on scriptural teachings about forgiveness, or learning conflict resolution strategies.

For many inmates, **fear of the unknown** is a significant psychological challenge. They may fear for their safety within the prison walls, or they may be anxious about the future, wondering how they will reintegrate into society upon release. Chaplains can address these fears by offering spiritual comfort and reassurance. By helping inmates connect with the deeper truths of their faith—whether it's trust in God's protection, the hope of redemption, or the belief in second chances—chaplains can help inmates build emotional resilience and face their fears with courage.

Loneliness, Isolation, and the Need for Connection

Prison life is often marked by profound **loneliness** and **isolation**. Many inmates are cut off from family, friends, and their previous social networks. This sense of disconnection can exacerbate feelings of despair and hopelessness. For some, the lack of meaningful relationships in prison may even lead to a spiritual crisis, as they feel abandoned not only by society but also by God.

Chaplains can address the psychological and spiritual need for **connection** by offering a consistent presence in the lives of inmates.

Whether through one-on-one visits, leading group worship services, or facilitating religious study groups, chaplains create spaces where inmates can experience **community** and **fellowship**. These relationships are crucial for inmates, as they often provide a lifeline to hope, healing, and faith.

In addition to providing personal connection, chaplains can encourage inmates to rebuild relationships with their **families** and **communities** outside of prison. For many inmates, the journey toward spiritual and emotional healing involves seeking reconciliation with those they have wronged. Chaplains can offer guidance on this path, helping inmates reflect on how they can repair broken relationships and make amends.

Spiritual Growth and Transformation

Finally, for some inmates, incarceration serves as a moment of profound **spiritual transformation**. Stripped of the distractions and temptations of their previous lives, they may turn to God or re-engage with their faith in a new way. Chaplains are in a unique position to nurture this spiritual awakening by offering guidance, spiritual mentorship, and resources for growth.

Inmates who experience spiritual transformation often express a renewed sense of **purpose**, seeing their incarceration as a turning point in their lives. Chaplains can encourage this growth by providing spiritual education, facilitating religious practices like prayer and worship, and offering counseling on how inmates can live out their faith within the prison environment and beyond.

For many inmates, this spiritual growth becomes a source of **hope** and **resilience** as they navigate the challenges of prison life. It may even inspire them to use their experiences to help others, whether through peer support, mentorship, or service within the prison community.

Conclusion

Incarceration presents profound spiritual and psychological challenges, but it can also be a time of deep reflection, healing, and transformation. Chaplains play a vital role in addressing the spiritual and emotional needs of inmates, offering them guidance, support, and hope in the midst of their struggles. By helping inmates navigate feelings of guilt, shame, anger, fear, and isolation, chaplains can facilitate personal and spiritual growth, leading inmates toward healing and redemption.

The chaplain's work in prisons is ultimately about offering a message of **hope**: no matter how dark the circumstances, inmates are not beyond the reach of God's grace. Through spiritual care and compassionate presence, chaplains help inmates discover that even in the most difficult of circumstances, there is the possibility for **meaning**, **purpose**, and a renewed sense of life.

Addressing Guilt, Forgiveness, and Reconciliation

Incarceration often forces individuals to confront the consequences of their actions, leading many prisoners to experience profound guilt and a deep need for forgiveness. For some, the burden of their past crimes or wrongdoings weighs heavily on their conscience, resulting in feelings of unworthiness, self-condemnation, and spiritual despair. At the same time, many prisoners long for reconciliation—not only with those they have harmed but also with their families, society, and themselves.

As chaplains minister to these individuals, they hold a unique responsibility in guiding prisoners through a difficult yet transformative journey of addressing guilt, seeking forgiveness, and pursuing reconciliation. This process is deeply spiritual, drawing on the belief that redemption is always possible and that broken relationships can be healed. This section explores how chaplains can facilitate this journey, providing spiritual guidance and support to inmates as they seek to confront their past and move toward healing.

The Burden of Guilt

Guilt is a complex and often overwhelming emotion for prisoners. For some, guilt arises from their recognition of the harm they have caused to others, whether through violent acts, betrayal, or neglect. For others, guilt may stem from deeper feelings of failure—toward their families, communities, or even God. This guilt can manifest as emotional distress, shame, and a sense of being unforgivable.

Left unchecked, guilt can spiral into self-destructive behaviors. It can foster a belief that the prisoner is irredeemable, leading to despair and hopelessness. This is why addressing guilt is so critical in the context of prison ministry.

Chaplains play a key role in helping prisoners confront their guilt in a way that is honest yet constructive. Rather than avoiding or denying the reality of their wrongdoing, prisoners must learn to acknowledge their guilt as a first step toward healing. Chaplains can facilitate this process through **pastoral counseling**, encouraging inmates to reflect on their actions with a spirit of accountability and self-awareness.

However, it is equally important that chaplains communicate the possibility of **forgiveness** and **redemption**. Guilt need not be a permanent burden; it can be a catalyst for change. Many faith traditions teach that while we are all flawed and sinful, we are also capable of transformation through divine grace. Chaplains can offer prisoners the assurance that no matter how grievous their past mistakes, they are not beyond the reach of God's mercy. This message of hope is essential in helping inmates move from guilt toward healing.

The Path to Forgiveness

Forgiveness is a powerful spiritual concept that lies at the heart of many religious traditions. For prisoners, the need for forgiveness is often multi-faceted: they may seek forgiveness from God, from the people they have harmed, and from themselves.

Seeking God's forgiveness is often the first step in a prisoner's spiritual journey toward healing. Chaplains can guide inmates through this process by helping them engage in repentance and prayer, offering scriptural teachings about God's mercy, and encouraging them to participate in religious practices that promote forgiveness, such as confession, prayer, or sacramental rites.

In Christian traditions, for example, the message of Jesus' forgiveness is central. Scriptures like 1 John 1:9 ("If we confess our sins, he is faithful and just to forgive us our sins and to cleanse us from all unrighteousness") can offer prisoners hope that they are not condemned to live in shame forever. Instead, they can receive forgiveness and begin anew. Chaplains may lead Bible studies, prayer services, or personal counseling sessions focused on themes of repentance, grace, and renewal.

However, **forgiving oneself** is often the most challenging aspect of the forgiveness process. Many prisoners, even after seeking God's forgiveness, continue to struggle with self-condemnation. They may believe that their actions were too terrible to ever truly be forgiven, or they may be haunted by the thought that they cannot undo the harm they have caused. Chaplains can offer compassionate support as prisoners navigate these internal struggles, helping them to understand that self-forgiveness is not about excusing their past, but about accepting God's grace and allowing themselves the opportunity to grow.

In their counseling roles, chaplains can use tools like **active listening** and **reflective questioning** to guide prisoners toward a place of greater self-acceptance. They may ask reflective questions that help inmates think about how they can change moving forward or what they can do to make amends for their past actions. This process of internal reconciliation is crucial for prisoners to experience emotional and spiritual freedom.

Reconciliation with Others

True healing for many prisoners involves seeking **reconciliation** with the people they have harmed. This is often the most painful and difficult part of the journey, as it requires prisoners to confront the real-world consequences of their actions and the suffering they have caused. However, reconciliation can also be the most transformative part of the forgiveness process.

Chaplains can guide inmates in understanding that while they cannot undo their past, they can take meaningful steps toward **restorative justice**—seeking to repair relationships and make amends for their wrongs. This process may include apologizing to their victims, writing letters of remorse, or participating in restorative justice programs that focus on healing and dialogue between offenders and victims.

Reconciliation may not always be possible in the literal sense. Victims may not be open to contact, or the harm may be too severe for direct engagement. In these cases, chaplains can still help prisoners to **pray** for their victims, to reflect on their wrongs, and to cultivate a spirit of **remorse** and **compassion** toward those they have hurt. This kind of spiritual reconciliation is crucial for prisoners' ongoing emotional and moral development.

At the same time, prisoners may need to seek reconciliation with their **families** and **communities**. Many inmates come from fractured family backgrounds, and their imprisonment may have further strained these relationships. Chaplains can offer guidance and counseling on how to rebuild trust and communication with family members, often encouraging prisoners to take small steps toward rebuilding relationships.

Healing Within the Prison Community

In addition to seeking reconciliation with those outside the prison walls, inmates can work toward healing within the prison community itself. Often, prison environments are marked by hostility, mistrust, and divisions. Chaplains can encourage prisoners to be agents of **peace** and **reconciliation** within these environments, fostering a spirit of cooperation and mutual respect. This can involve participating in group worship, prayer circles, or conflict resolution programs.

By promoting reconciliation within the prison, chaplains help create a more supportive and healing atmosphere where inmates can work together toward mutual healing and growth.

Conclusion

The journey from guilt to forgiveness and reconciliation is both a personal and spiritual transformation. For prisoners, this journey is often long and difficult, requiring them to face the pain of their past actions and the consequences of their choices. However, through the compassionate guidance of chaplains, inmates can find a path toward healing—one that leads to spiritual freedom, personal growth, and the possibility of reconciliation.

Chaplains, grounded in their faith and committed to the principles of mercy, grace, and redemption, are uniquely positioned to facilitate this process. By offering spiritual counsel, fostering environments of trust, and helping prisoners see the possibility of forgiveness, chaplains play a critical role in helping individuals find peace within themselves and begin the process of restoring broken relationships. Through this work, the message of **hope**, **grace**, and **renewal** is carried into the darkest corners of incarceration, offering prisoners the possibility of true transformation and healing.

Navigating Challenges Within Prison Systems

Prison chaplaincy presents a unique set of challenges, requiring chaplains to navigate complex institutional dynamics, security concerns, and diverse worldviews—including atheism and postmodern perspectives that deny or question the existence of God. Chaplains working in this environment must balance the demands of the prison system with their call to provide spiritual care to inmates, many of whom may be skeptical or hostile toward faith. The challenge is compounded by the postmodern worldview that dismisses absolute truths and often regards religion as an irrelevant relic of the past.

Despite these challenges, chaplains can engage with inmates meaningfully by addressing their spiritual, psychological, and emotional needs while standing firm in theological soundness. This chapter explores how chaplains can navigate institutional resistance, earn the trust of inmates, and respond to secular and atheist perspectives with wisdom, grace, and compassion.

Institutional Resistance and Security Concerns

Prison chaplains frequently face resistance from within the institution itself. Prisons are environments driven by rules, security protocols, and a focus on maintaining order. In such settings, spiritual care may be perceived as secondary to the primary goals of confinement, discipline, and security. Chaplains may encounter resistance in the following ways:

- **Restricted Access to Inmates**: Chaplains may face limited opportunities to interact with inmates due to tight security measures or strict schedules.

- **Skepticism from Prison Staff**: Some staff members, particularly those with secular or atheistic views, may question the relevance of chaplaincy in a punitive system and see spiritual care as unnecessary.
- **Bureaucratic Obstacles**: Gaining approval for religious programs or access to certain prison areas may involve navigating complicated bureaucratic processes.

To overcome these hurdles, chaplains must demonstrate the value of their work. By showing how spiritual care can contribute to the broader goals of rehabilitation, improved inmate behavior, and emotional healing, chaplains can gain the support of prison administrators. Moreover, understanding the importance of security concerns can help chaplains find creative ways to provide spiritual care that aligns with institutional rules, such as offering one-on-one sessions or written materials when group services are not possible.

Building Trust with Inmates

Incarcerated individuals often carry deep mistrust toward authority figures, including chaplains. Many have been let down by people in positions of power throughout their lives—whether it be family, teachers, or law enforcement. This history of betrayal can make it difficult for inmates to open up to chaplains, who are seen as part of the prison system. Building trust is a slow and deliberate process, requiring consistent, compassionate engagement.

One of the most effective ways to build trust is through **active listening**. Inmates often feel unheard or disregarded, and chaplains can offer a powerful counterpoint by providing a safe space for them to express their fears, doubts, and regrets without judgment. Empathy is crucial in this setting; chaplains must approach each inmate with compassion, recognizing their inherent dignity and worth as human beings.

Confidentiality also plays a key role in building trust. Inmates must feel confident that what they share with the chaplain will remain private. This assurance encourages them to open up about their deepest struggles, including guilt, shame, and spiritual doubts.

The Challenge of Postmodernity and Atheism: Engaging Skeptical Inmates

In the modern prison environment, chaplains frequently encounter the influence of **postmodernity** and **atheism**. Postmodern thought, which emphasizes relativism and the rejection of absolute truths, can lead inmates to view religious beliefs as outdated or irrelevant. Atheists, who deny the existence of God outright, may see little value in the spiritual care offered by chaplains.

For chaplains, engaging with skeptical or atheist inmates requires a thoughtful, respectful approach. This engagement should not be about winning arguments but about planting seeds of reflection and offering a space where deeper questions about life and meaning can be explored. Inmates who reject traditional religious beliefs may still grapple with spiritual questions, even if they don't use religious language to express them. Chaplains can gently challenge their assumptions by posing rhetorical questions that invite reflection:

- **Is it possible that the human heart's yearning for meaning, justice, and purpose points to something greater than ourselves?**
- **Why do we feel a deep sense of right and wrong if morality is merely a social construct with no absolute basis?**
- **Can a purely materialistic view of the world fully explain the human experience of love, sacrifice, and hope?**

- **What if forgiveness and redemption are real possibilities, regardless of past mistakes?**
- **In the face of suffering, is it not at least worth considering that there might be a God who cares, even when life feels unfair or cruel?**

These questions are not meant to coerce or corner inmates into a religious commitment, but to awaken their innate curiosity about the deeper questions of existence that often emerge in moments of crisis or despair. Many inmates wrestle with guilt, shame, and a desire for meaning, even if they reject traditional religious answers. By providing a compassionate and non-confrontational space for these conversations, chaplains can offer inmates the opportunity to explore spiritual realities in a way that feels relevant and meaningful.

Responding to the Postmodern Mindset

For those shaped by postmodernism, the rejection of absolute truth can lead to a deep sense of **spiritual disconnection**. Inmates may believe that religion is merely one perspective among many, no more valid than their own personal experiences. As a result, chaplains may encounter resistance to ideas of objective morality, sin, or redemption.

To respond to the postmodern mindset, chaplains must:

- **Emphasize Shared Human Longings**: While postmodernism rejects universal truths, it cannot deny the shared human experiences of longing for connection, forgiveness, and hope. Chaplains can focus on these universal themes, offering a message of grace and redemption that speaks to the heart's deepest desires.
- **Respect Individual Autonomy**: Postmodern thought prizes individual autonomy and the right to define one's own reality. Chaplains can respect this autonomy by offering spiritual guidance in a way that empowers inmates to explore faith on their own terms, without pressure or coercion.

- **Maintain Theological Soundness**: Despite the challenges of postmodern skepticism, chaplains must remain theologically grounded, offering a clear and compelling presentation of the Gospel. This does not mean forcing religious beliefs on inmates but rather being ready to articulate the hope, forgiveness, and transformation that faith offers.

Theological Soundness: Relevance in a Secular World

In an increasingly secular and postmodern world, it is more important than ever for chaplains to maintain **theological soundness**. Chaplains must be confident in their own faith and equipped to offer clear, compassionate answers to inmates' spiritual struggles. This means being rooted in scripture, understanding the core tenets of faith, and presenting them in a way that is both relevant and respectful of the diverse worldviews inmates hold.

A theologically sound chaplain is able to provide guidance on issues like guilt, forgiveness, and reconciliation, helping inmates navigate their spiritual journey while offering a path to redemption that transcends the relativism of postmodernity. In this context, chaplains can:

- **Offer the Hope of Absolute Truth**: While postmodernity denies absolute truth, the message of the Gospel offers the certainty of God's love, grace, and redemption. For many inmates, this message provides the hope and purpose they desperately seek.
- **Challenge Atheism with Love and Grace**: While atheists may reject the idea of God, chaplains can still provide compassionate care, demonstrating through their actions the love and grace that reflect God's character. Over time, this witness can open doors for deeper spiritual conversations.

Conclusion

Prison chaplaincy presents a complex set of challenges, from navigating institutional resistance and security concerns to engaging with inmates shaped by postmodernity and atheism. Chaplains must remain theologically grounded, equipped with the skills and sensitivity to engage with these diverse perspectives while advocating for the spiritual and emotional well-being of inmates. By building trust, respecting individual autonomy, and offering a compassionate, non-judgmental presence, chaplains can help inmates explore the deeper questions of life and faith, providing hope and healing in a setting where such gifts are often in short supply.

Conducting Services and Bible Studies in Prison

One of the primary roles of a prison chaplain is to provide regular spiritual services and Bible studies that foster a sense of community, offer spiritual nourishment, and help inmates grow in their faith. This ministry work is not just about preaching sermons or leading prayers; it's about creating an atmosphere where inmates can experience transformation, healing, and hope in the midst of their circumstances

Prison is a place where isolation, guilt, and shame often dominate the emotional landscape, so spiritual services and Bible studies provide a rare opportunity for inmates to connect with something greater than themselves, to reflect on their lives, and to experience the grace of God. However, leading these sessions in a prison setting comes with unique challenges, requiring chaplains to adapt their approach to meet the spiritual and emotional needs of the incarcerated.

1. Creating an Inclusive and Welcoming Environment

In a prison setting, chaplains will often encounter a diverse group of individuals—some from different denominations, others from different religious backgrounds, and still others who may not profess any faith at all. It is important to create an environment where everyone feels welcome, regardless of their beliefs.

Respect for Diversity: While the Bible may be the central text in many services and studies, chaplains must be sensitive to the fact that not every inmate will share the same understanding or interpretation of scripture. Chaplains should emphasize universal spiritual themes like forgiveness, redemption, hope, and restoration, which resonate with all human beings, regardless of their religious background.

Tone of Invitation, Not Coercion: Chaplains should invite inmates to participate in services and Bible studies with a tone of openness, rather than making them feel obligated or pressured to attend. Offering inmates a space to explore faith without judgment allows them to come forward with genuine interest, rather than out of a sense of duty or fear.

2. Meeting Inmates Where They Are

Inmates come to spiritual services and Bible studies at various stages of life and faith. Some may have been involved in church communities before their incarceration, while others may be encountering Christian teachings for the first time. Chaplains must be prepared to meet inmates where they are on their spiritual journey and guide them forward, regardless of their starting point.

Simplifying Complex Concepts: Many inmates may have little experience with formal theology or Bible study. Therefore, it is important to explain complex theological concepts in simple and relatable terms. Avoid using jargon or overly technical language, and focus instead on practical applications of faith that address the struggles and challenges inmates face in their daily lives.

Encouraging Vulnerability: The prison environment fosters an attitude of toughness and emotional withdrawal, yet spiritual growth requires vulnerability. Chaplains can model vulnerability through their own authenticity and honesty, encouraging inmates to be open about their struggles, doubts, and fears in a safe and supportive setting.

3. Structuring Services and Bible Studies

Chaplains should approach the structure of their services and Bible studies with intentionality, ensuring that these sessions are both meaningful and manageable within the constraints of the prison setting. Whether leading a weekly worship service or facilitating a Bible study, chaplains can use a structure that allows for spiritual engagement, reflection, and community-building.

Opening with Prayer and Worship: Most services or Bible studies should begin with a time of prayer, which helps to center the group and set the tone for spiritual reflection. Depending on the resources available, chaplains may include a time of singing or worship. Music can be a powerful way to create an atmosphere of worship and to bring inmates together in a communal act of praise.

Scripture Reading and Reflection: Choose passages of scripture that resonate with the particular struggles inmates face—whether those passages deal with forgiveness, suffering, hope, or renewal. After reading the passage, offer a reflection that connects the text to the inmates' lived experience. For example, stories of biblical figures who experienced imprisonment (like Joseph, Paul, or even Jesus) can provide relatable and inspiring examples of faith during hardship.

Interactive Bible Study: Bible studies should be interactive, giving inmates the opportunity to ask questions, share their thoughts, and engage in discussion. Encourage participation by asking open-ended questions and prompting inmates to reflect on how the scripture applies to their lives. Be prepared to answer questions, but also acknowledge when a question requires deeper thought or exploration. This creates a learning environment where dialogue and exploration are welcomed.

Personal Testimonies: If possible, encourage inmates to share their personal testimonies during services or Bible studies. Testimonies can be powerful examples of God's work in individuals' lives and can inspire others to seek transformation. Creating space for testimonies helps build community and allows inmates to feel heard and valued within the group.

4. Offering Hope and Encouragement

Inmates often struggle with feelings of guilt, shame, and hopelessness, especially when faced with the consequences of their actions. Spiritual services and Bible studies provide a unique opportunity to offer hope and encouragement. Chaplains should emphasize the message of God's unconditional love, the possibility of redemption, and the hope of a future that is not defined by past mistakes.

The Gospel of Forgiveness: Many inmates wrestle with deep feelings of guilt and the belief that they are beyond forgiveness. Chaplains can remind them that the Gospel offers grace and mercy to all, no matter their past. By focusing on the themes of repentance and redemption found in scripture, chaplains can help inmates realize that they are never too far from God's love and forgiveness.

Hope in the Midst of Suffering: For inmates dealing with long sentences, difficult conditions, or the weight of their actions, it can be easy to lose hope. Chaplains can draw upon biblical examples of endurance and perseverance, such as the stories of Job or Paul, to remind inmates that God is with them even in their suffering and that they are not alone.

5. Building a Spiritual Community

One of the most powerful aspects of spiritual services and Bible studies is the sense of community they can foster among inmates. In an environment where trust is often broken and individuals feel isolated, the chaplain's role is to help inmates see that they are part of something larger—a spiritual family.

Encouraging Peer Support: Chaplains can encourage inmates to support one another in their spiritual journeys. When inmates feel connected to a community, they are more likely to engage in positive behaviors and to find meaning and purpose in their daily lives. Chaplains should facilitate opportunities for inmates to share their struggles and victories, creating a sense of mutual encouragement and accountability.

Promoting Reconciliation: Services and Bible studies can also provide a forum for reconciliation among inmates. In an environment marked by conflict, anger, and division, chaplains can promote forgiveness and healing within the inmate population. By addressing themes of reconciliation in scripture and offering practical steps for resolving conflicts, chaplains can contribute to a more peaceful and supportive prison community.

6. One-on-One Sessions for Deeper Engagement

In addition to group services and Bible studies, chaplains often conduct one-on-one sessions with inmates who are seeking spiritual guidance or who may not feel comfortable participating in group activities. These individual sessions offer a chance for deeper engagement, personalized support, and focused discipleship.

Listening and Counseling: Chaplains should prioritize active listening during one-on-one sessions, allowing inmates to share their concerns, doubts, and personal struggles. Many inmates will need spiritual and emotional counseling to address issues such as guilt, trauma, and broken relationships.

Guided Scripture Study: Chaplains can use these sessions to offer personalized Bible study, guiding inmates through passages of scripture that speak to their individual circumstances. This one-on-one time allows for deeper theological discussions and a more tailored spiritual journey.

Prayer and Pastoral Care: Closing one-on-one sessions with prayer provides comfort and reinforces the chaplain's role as a spiritual guide. Offering to pray with and for inmates helps build trust and deepens their connection to the chaplain's ministry.

Conclusion

Conducting spiritual services and Bible studies in prison is one of the most impactful ways chaplains can minister to inmates. Through these gatherings, chaplains offer not only spiritual nourishment but also the possibility of transformation and healing. By creating a welcoming environment, addressing the spiritual needs of inmates, and fostering a sense of community, chaplains can help inmates experience the redemptive power of faith even in the most challenging circumstances.

Reintegration and Healing Post-Incarceration

The journey of an inmate does not end upon release from prison; instead, it marks the beginning of a challenging transition back into society. As a vital part of this process, prison chaplains play a key role in preparing inmates for reintegration, helping them rebuild their lives with a new spiritual and moral foundation. This process of reintegration is not merely about adjusting to life outside prison walls; it encompasses the emotional, psychological, and spiritual healing necessary to foster resilience and hope in a world that may feel foreign and unwelcoming.

1. Understanding the Challenges of Reintegration

Inmates face a myriad of challenges when re-entering society, including stigma, lack of employment opportunities, fractured relationships, and a struggle to adapt to life outside the confines of prison. Many may carry deep feelings of guilt or shame from their past actions, leading to self-doubt and a diminished sense of self-worth.

Societal Stigma: The stigma associated with incarceration can create barriers to reintegration, making it difficult for former inmates to secure jobs, housing, and social support. Chaplains can help inmates navigate these challenges by providing encouragement and resources to build a new life.

Emotional and Psychological Struggles: Many inmates experience anxiety, depression, or trauma as they transition back into society. This psychological burden can lead to feelings of isolation and hopelessness. Chaplains can offer support and counseling to help inmates process these emotions and build coping strategies.

2. Building a Support Network

A crucial component of successful reintegration is the establishment of a strong support network. Chaplains can help inmates identify and connect with community resources that facilitate this support, ensuring that they do not have to navigate the challenges of reintegration alone.

Connection to Local Churches and Faith Communities: Chaplains can facilitate introductions to local churches or faith communities that are welcoming to former inmates. These connections provide spiritual support, friendship, and accountability, helping individuals establish a sense of belonging.

Engaging with Community Programs: Many communities have programs specifically designed to assist formerly incarcerated individuals. Chaplains can educate inmates about these resources, which may include job training, counseling, housing assistance, and mentorship programs. Helping inmates access these resources can significantly ease their transition.

Encouraging Healthy Relationships: Reintegration also involves rebuilding relationships with family and friends. Chaplains can offer guidance on how to approach these reconnections, helping inmates navigate the complexities of forgiveness and reconciliation. Family counseling sessions may also be beneficial, allowing for open communication and healing.

3. Spiritual Foundations for Reintegration

A strong spiritual foundation can provide the necessary strength and resilience for inmates as they reintegrate into society. Chaplains have a unique opportunity to foster spiritual growth during the re-entry process, helping inmates develop a deeper understanding of their faith and its practical application in their daily lives.

Encouraging Personal Reflection: Chaplains can facilitate personal reflection by encouraging inmates to journal their thoughts, feelings, and prayers. This practice can help them process their experiences, recognize patterns in their lives, and set spiritual goals for the future.

Establishing Spiritual Disciplines: Chaplains can teach former inmates the importance of spiritual disciplines such as prayer, meditation, and Bible study as tools for maintaining a strong spiritual life. These practices can offer a sense of purpose, direction, and comfort in times of difficulty.

Fostering Accountability and Mentorship: The support of a mentor or spiritual advisor can be invaluable during the reintegration process. Chaplains can act as mentors themselves or connect former inmates with other individuals who can provide accountability, encouragement, and spiritual guidance.

4. Addressing the Need for Forgiveness and Healing

The journey of reintegration often involves confronting past actions, seeking forgiveness, and allowing space for healing. Chaplains can guide inmates through this process, emphasizing the importance of both seeking forgiveness from others and extending forgiveness to oneself.

Facilitating Forgiveness: Chaplains can help inmates understand the transformative power of forgiveness. They can offer counseling on how to approach individuals they may have wronged, as well as how to seek forgiveness from God. By fostering an attitude of forgiveness, inmates can let go of guilt and embrace a new identity.

Processing Trauma: Many inmates carry trauma from their past experiences, whether from their time in prison or their life before incarceration. Chaplains can provide a safe space for inmates to process these traumatic experiences, guiding them toward healing and emotional well-being.

Encouraging New Beginnings: Reintegration is also an opportunity for new beginnings. Chaplains can help inmates recognize that their past does not define them and that they have the power to shape their future. By emphasizing God's grace and the concept of new life in Christ, chaplains can instill hope for a brighter tomorrow.

5. Continuing the Journey of Growth

Reintegration is not a one-time event but a continuous journey of growth and development. Chaplains can help former inmates establish goals and plans for their future, encouraging them to pursue education, employment, and healthy relationships as they build their new lives.

Setting Goals: Helping inmates identify short-term and long-term goals can provide them with a sense of purpose and direction. Whether seeking employment, enrolling in educational programs, or pursuing personal development, chaplains can assist inmates in creating actionable plans.

Celebrating Milestones: Celebrating achievements, no matter how small, can boost self-esteem and reinforce positive behaviors. Chaplains can organize events or gatherings that recognize milestones in the reintegration journey, providing an opportunity for community support and encouragement.

Ongoing Spiritual Engagement: Encourage former inmates to stay engaged in their faith communities and continue their spiritual growth. Regular church attendance, participation in Bible studies, and involvement in ministry can help maintain their spiritual foundation and provide ongoing support.

Conclusion

The role of the prison chaplain extends far beyond the walls of the institution. By actively engaging in the reintegration process, chaplains can make a profound difference in the lives of former inmates, guiding them toward healing, hope, and new beginnings. Through building a support network, establishing spiritual foundations, facilitating forgiveness, and encouraging personal growth, chaplains can help individuals transition into society as transformed and empowered individuals, ready to embrace a future filled with possibilities.

CHAPTER 4

Hospital Chaplaincy

Ministry in a Healthcare Environment

The hospital is a place where the fragility of human life is most apparent—a space where sickness, suffering, trauma, and the uncertainty of life and death converge. For patients, families, and even healthcare workers, it can be a time of profound vulnerability, fear, and emotional exhaustion. In this context, chaplains play a crucial role, offering spiritual care, comfort, and guidance amid the physical suffering that pervades the environment.

Healthcare chaplaincy is a ministry of presence and support, where chaplains walk alongside individuals as they navigate some of life's most difficult moments. Unlike traditional pastoral roles within a church setting, the chaplain's ministry in a healthcare environment is often transient, unpredictable, and deeply intimate, requiring sensitivity, flexibility, and a profound understanding of human suffering.

1. Providing Spiritual Care in Times of Crisis

In a hospital setting, chaplains are often called upon during moments of crisis—when a loved one has just received a devastating diagnosis, when a patient is undergoing life-saving surgery, or when the possibility of death is imminent. These moments require chaplains to be a steadying presence, providing spiritual care that addresses both immediate emotional needs and long-term existential questions.

Being a Non-Anxious Presence: In times of crisis, emotions can run high, and uncertainty can fuel anxiety and fear. Chaplains are called to be a non-anxious presence, offering calm and reassurance even when answers are elusive. This requires the chaplain to manage their own emotions and remain grounded in their faith, serving as a source of stability for others.

Offering Hope Without False Promises: In moments of uncertainty, chaplains must strike a delicate balance between offering hope and avoiding false promises. Hope, in a spiritual sense, is not always about the assurance of a physical cure; sometimes, it is about finding peace, meaning, and a sense of divine presence even in the face of suffering. Chaplains can help individuals find that deeper hope by connecting them to their faith and spiritual beliefs.

Ministering Across Religious Backgrounds: Hospitals are places of diversity, where patients and families may come from various religious and spiritual traditions. A skilled chaplain can offer spiritual care that is sensitive to different belief systems, whether that involves leading a Christian in prayer, providing a moment of silence for a patient of another faith, or simply being present for those who claim no religious affiliation but still seek comfort.

2. Supporting Patients Through Illness and Suffering

For patients, illness is often a time of deep introspection and spiritual questioning. Why is this happening to me? What is the purpose of my suffering? Is there something beyond this life? As a chaplain, providing spiritual care involves helping patients wrestle with these difficult questions, finding meaning in their experience, and connecting them to a sense of hope and peace.

Listening to Their Story: Often, the most important thing a chaplain can do is simply listen. Patients may be grappling with complex emotions—fear, anger, guilt, or despair—and need a safe space to express their feelings. Through active listening, chaplains can validate these emotions and create a sense of connection that allows patients to feel heard and understood.

Guiding Through Spiritual Questions: Many patients turn to spiritual beliefs in times of illness, searching for answers to existential questions about life, death, and the afterlife. Chaplains can provide gentle guidance, helping patients explore their faith and find comfort in their beliefs. For Christian patients, scripture and prayer may offer solace, while patients of other faiths may need support that aligns with their spiritual traditions.

Finding Meaning in Suffering: One of the greatest challenges of ministry in a healthcare environment is addressing the question of suffering. While chaplains cannot remove the physical pain or illness a patient is experiencing, they can help individuals find meaning within their suffering. For some, this may involve understanding suffering as part of a larger spiritual journey; for others, it may be about reconciling with God or accepting their circumstances with grace and trust.

3. Caring for Families and Loved Ones

Chaplains in hospitals often find that their ministry extends beyond the patients to the families and loved ones who accompany them. Watching a loved one suffer can be as painful as enduring the illness itself, and families often need emotional and spiritual support to cope with their feelings of helplessness, grief, and fear.

Supporting During Times of Loss: When a patient's condition deteriorates or death seems imminent, families may need a chaplain's guidance through the process of grief and loss. Whether sitting in silence, offering a prayer, or simply being a compassionate presence, chaplains can help families begin to process their grief and find comfort in their faith.

Facilitating Communication: In some cases, families may be unsure how to communicate with each other or with the patient during times of illness. Chaplains can help facilitate difficult conversations—whether about end-of-life decisions, unresolved conflicts, or spiritual concerns—allowing families to express their emotions and find closure.

Providing Pastoral Counseling: Many family members experience a crisis of faith when a loved one becomes ill. They may question why God would allow such suffering or feel abandoned by their faith in the face of tragedy. Chaplains can provide pastoral counseling to help them navigate these spiritual struggles, encouraging them to lean on their faith rather than abandon it during difficult times.

4. Ministering to Healthcare Workers

Chaplains in a healthcare environment are not only there for patients and families but also for the healthcare workers who provide care. Doctors, nurses, and other medical staff experience significant emotional strain as they care for the sick and dying on a daily basis. The constant exposure to trauma, death, and suffering can lead to burnout, compassion fatigue, and moral distress.

Providing Emotional and Spiritual Support: Chaplains can offer a listening ear and spiritual guidance to healthcare workers who may be struggling with the emotional toll of their work. By creating opportunities for conversation, prayer, or even just a quiet moment of reflection, chaplains can help healthcare workers process their emotions and reconnect with their own sense of purpose.

Offering Respite: Chaplains can also provide moments of respite for healthcare workers who are feeling overwhelmed or exhausted. Whether it's a brief prayer before a difficult procedure or a conversation in the break room, chaplains can create sacred spaces where healthcare professionals can pause, breathe, and regain their emotional and spiritual strength.

Ethical Consultation and Support: Healthcare workers often face ethical dilemmas, especially in end-of-life care, where decisions about treatment and patient autonomy can conflict with spiritual or moral values. Chaplains can offer ethical support by helping medical staff navigate these difficult decisions in a way that honors both the patient's wishes and the spiritual beliefs of all involved.

5. Navigating Ethical Dilemmas in Healthcare

Ethical dilemmas are a common occurrence in healthcare settings, particularly when dealing with issues like end-of-life care, patient autonomy, and medical decisions that may conflict with a patient's or family's spiritual beliefs. Chaplains are often called upon to provide spiritual and moral guidance in these situations, helping patients, families, and healthcare teams make decisions that align with both ethical principles and spiritual values.

Respecting Patient Autonomy: Chaplains must navigate the delicate balance between honoring a patient's spiritual beliefs and supporting their right to make autonomous decisions about their care. Whether a patient chooses to continue aggressive treatment or opt for palliative care, chaplains can provide spiritual support that respects their choices while offering comfort and guidance.

Supporting Families Through Ethical Conflicts: Families may experience conflicts about what constitutes appropriate care for a loved one, especially when religious or cultural beliefs come into play. Chaplains can mediate these conversations, helping families understand the medical realities while supporting their spiritual and emotional needs. In some cases, chaplains may also help families come to terms with decisions that seem contrary to their religious expectations, such as the withdrawal of life-sustaining treatment.

Collaborating with Healthcare Teams: Chaplains often serve as a bridge between the medical team and the patient or family, offering insight into the spiritual and ethical concerns that might influence care decisions. By working collaboratively with doctors, nurses, and social workers, chaplains can ensure that spiritual values are respected while providing holistic care that meets the physical, emotional, and spiritual needs of the patient.

6. Conducting Bedside Rituals and Sacraments

In a healthcare environment, chaplains are frequently asked to perform religious rituals, prayers, and sacraments at the bedside. These sacred moments can provide patients and families with a sense of comfort and connection to their faith, offering spiritual nourishment even in times of physical suffering.

Administering Sacraments: For Christian patients, sacraments like communion, anointing of the sick, and last rites are important elements of spiritual care. Chaplains should be prepared to administer these sacraments in a respectful and reverent manner, bringing the presence of God into the hospital room.

Offering Prayers and Blessings: Whether patients are seeking healing, peace, or comfort, chaplains can offer prayers that reflect their specific needs and faith traditions. Prayers for healing, strength, and hope can uplift patients and their families, offering a sense of divine presence in the midst of suffering.

Creating Sacred Space: Chaplains can also create sacred spaces in the hospital room through the use of symbols, prayers, or silence. These moments of reverence allow patients and families to experience the presence of the divine, even in a clinical setting, and can provide peace during times of uncertainty and fear.

Conclusion

The ministry of chaplains in a healthcare environment is one of profound compassion, presence, and spiritual care. Whether supporting patients through illness and suffering, comforting families in times of crisis, or providing emotional and spiritual guidance to healthcare workers, chaplains serve as beacons of hope and faith in the midst of pain and uncertainty. Through their ministry, chaplains offer more than just spiritual care—they offer a reminder of the divine presence that transcends even the most difficult moments of human life.

Supporting Patients and Their Families

Hospital chaplaincy often requires navigating some of the most challenging moments in the lives of patients and their families—times of difficult decisions, terminal illness, and the approach of death. In these moments, the chaplain's role is not just to offer practical support but to be a source of deep emotional and spiritual care. Whether facing a terminal diagnosis, contemplating end-of-life choices, or enduring the pain of grief, patients and their families need compassion, guidance, and—most importantly—hope.

1. The Power of Hope in the Midst of Suffering

Hope is one of the most profound spiritual gifts a chaplain can offer to both patients and families. For the patient, hope does not always mean the expectation of a physical cure; instead, it can mean the assurance that their life has meaning, that they are loved, and that they are not alone in their suffering. Even in the face of terminal illness, hope can manifest as peace, reconciliation, or the belief in a life beyond this one.

For families, hope often takes the form of emotional strength and spiritual resilience. As they watch their loved ones endure illness or prepare for death, families may feel overwhelmed with fear, grief, or helplessness. In these moments, a chaplain can help them find hope—not in the avoidance of suffering, but in the possibility of spiritual healing, reconciliation, and the presence of God's grace throughout the journey.

By helping patients and families tap into a deeper sense of hope, chaplains provide a powerful spiritual anchor in the midst of uncertainty and fear. This hope can come in many forms:

Hope for Healing: While medical outcomes are not always within control, chaplains can encourage patients and families to seek healing on a spiritual and emotional level. Healing doesn't always mean the absence of disease; it can mean finding inner peace, reconciling with loved ones, or deepening one's faith.

Hope for Meaning: Illness and suffering can feel chaotic and meaningless, but chaplains help patients and families uncover a sense of purpose even in these trying times. Whether it's a renewed connection to faith, the opportunity to reconcile broken relationships, or simply the act of sharing love and memories, finding meaning brings comfort.

Hope in the Afterlife: For many patients and families, hope is found in the belief that death is not the end, but a transition to eternal life. Chaplains can provide prayers, scripture, and spiritual guidance that affirms the patient's belief in an afterlife, offering hope beyond the boundaries of physical existence.

2. Compassionate Presence in Times of Grief

For patients and families grappling with terminal illness, grief is a constant companion. As chaplains, one of the most essential ways to support them is through the ministry of presence—a quiet, compassionate, and non-judgmental presence that allows people to express their deepest fears and grief without feeling rushed or dismissed.

Listening with Empathy: In moments of crisis, words are often insufficient to address the depth of pain and sorrow. Sometimes, the most important thing a chaplain can do is simply listen, offering patients and families a space to voice their grief, fear, and doubts. Active listening helps them feel heard and understood, which in turn allows them to begin processing their emotions.

Providing Spiritual Counseling: Families often struggle with their faith in the face of illness or impending death. They may question why God allows suffering or feel anger at what seems like the injustice of losing a loved one. Chaplains can provide spiritual counseling that addresses these concerns, helping families find solace in their faith even when they are grappling with deep pain.

Facilitating Family Communication: As families face difficult choices, such as discontinuing life-sustaining treatment or preparing for a loved one's passing, communication can break down due to emotional strain. Chaplains can act as mediators, helping families talk through their fears, regrets, or disagreements with compassion and understanding. This helps families unite during difficult moments, allowing for healing conversations that foster peace and reconciliation.

3. Offering Prayers and Spiritual Rituals for Comfort

In times of illness and death, spiritual rituals provide patients and families with a tangible sense of connection to the divine. Chaplains are often called upon to perform prayers, sacraments, and other rituals that bring comfort, especially when death feels near.

Bedside Prayers: Simple prayers at the bedside, whether for healing, peace, or guidance, offer patients and families a moment of quiet reflection and connection to their faith. These prayers can soothe emotional and spiritual anxiety, reminding them of God's presence and care.

Sacraments and Last Rites: For patients approaching the end of life, sacraments such as anointing of the sick, communion, or last rites provide a profound sense of spiritual completeness. These rituals help the patient find peace in the knowledge that they are spiritually prepared to meet God, offering comfort to both the patient and their family.

Creating Sacred Space: Chaplains can also help transform a hospital room into a sacred space by offering blessings, scripture readings, or moments of silence. This allows families to experience a sense of reverence and divine presence, even in a clinical setting, which can bring deep spiritual comfort.

4. Helping Families Prepare for the Dying Process

For many families, watching a loved one die is one of the most painful experiences they will ever endure. Chaplains provide essential support by helping them prepare—both emotionally and spiritually—for the dying process.

Explaining the Dying Process: Chaplains, in collaboration with medical staff, can help families understand the physical stages of dying, offering reassurance that what they are witnessing is part of the natural process. By demystifying death and offering spiritual guidance, chaplains help families cope with the physical changes their loved ones are undergoing.

Encouraging Final Conversations: As death approaches, chaplains encourage families to have meaningful conversations with their loved ones—expressing love, offering forgiveness, and sharing final moments together. These conversations, though difficult, allow for closure and can bring peace to both the patient and their family.

Providing Grief Support: After a loved one passes, the chaplain's role shifts to providing ongoing grief support. Whether through follow-up visits, prayer, or connecting families with grief counseling resources, chaplains ensure that families are not left alone to navigate their sorrow. Offering compassionate presence during these early stages of grief is essential for long-term healing.

5. Supporting Healthcare Workers

In addition to supporting patients and families, chaplains are also a valuable resource for healthcare workers, who face immense emotional and spiritual strain while caring for terminally ill patients. Healthcare workers often experience grief, moral distress, and compassion fatigue as they witness suffering and death. Chaplains provide an outlet for these emotions by offering pastoral care, prayers, and a space for reflection.

Providing Emotional Support: Healthcare workers may turn to chaplains for help processing their own emotional reactions to patient deaths or difficult ethical decisions. Chaplains offer a safe and confidential space for medical professionals to express their feelings, helping them cope with the emotional toll of their work.

Offering Spiritual Guidance: For healthcare workers with strong religious or spiritual beliefs, chaplains can offer guidance on how to integrate faith into their professional lives, providing reassurance that their work is a ministry of healing and compassion.

Conclusion: A Ministry of Hope

At the heart of a chaplain's work in healthcare is the power of hope. Whether offering prayers for healing, facilitating meaningful conversations, or simply being a calm presence, chaplains help patients and families see that even in the midst of suffering, there is hope. This hope may not always come in the form of physical recovery, but it manifests in the deeper assurance of peace, reconciliation, and the abiding presence of God. Through their ministry, chaplains provide a path forward—one illuminated by faith, comfort, and the eternal promise that no one faces the journey of illness and death alone.

Navigating Ethical Dilemmas

In healthcare settings, chaplains often encounter ethical dilemmas that arise from the complex interplay between medical decisions and spiritual beliefs. These situations can be particularly challenging because they require chaplains to act as spiritual advisors, mediators, and advocates, all while navigating delicate emotional and ethical terrain. At times, a patient's or family's religious convictions may conflict with the medical advice being given, creating tension between the pursuit of medical care and adherence to deeply held beliefs. Chaplains must be prepared to address these conflicts with sensitivity, wisdom, and theological soundness.

1. Understanding Ethical Dilemmas in Healthcare

Ethical dilemmas in healthcare typically arise when the values, beliefs, or priorities of the patient or family clash with the medical recommendations of healthcare providers. These dilemmas may involve issues such as:

- **End-of-life care decisions**: Questions of withdrawing or withholding life support, administering palliative care, or pursuing aggressive treatments at the end of life.
- **Religious opposition to medical interventions**: For example, some religious traditions may prohibit blood transfusions, certain surgical procedures, or the use of specific medications.
- **Medical decisions for incapacitated patients**: When patients are unable to make decisions for themselves, families may struggle with making choices on their behalf, especially if religious beliefs are involved.
- **Reproductive health and abortion**: Some patients may face ethical conflicts related to reproductive health, such as fertility treatments, contraception, or abortion, due to their religious beliefs.
- **Conflicts between patient autonomy and healthcare policies**: In some cases, hospital policies or state regulations may limit patient choices, leading to ethical challenges for patients whose religious or personal beliefs demand a different course of action.

As mediators of faith and spiritual caregivers, chaplains are often called upon to help patients and families navigate these difficult situations while also considering the medical professionals' concerns and the limitations of medical care.

2. Balancing Medical Realities and Spiritual Beliefs

Chaplains work at the intersection of spiritual beliefs and medical realities, which can sometimes seem at odds with one another. In moments of crisis, patients or families may cling tightly to religious convictions, especially when facing life-and-death decisions. Chaplains must skillfully balance respect for these spiritual beliefs with the realities of the patient's medical condition, providing counsel that honors both.

a. Facilitating Open Communication

One of the chaplain's most essential roles in navigating ethical dilemmas is to facilitate open, compassionate communication between patients, families, and healthcare providers. Misunderstandings or conflicts often arise due to poor communication or a lack of understanding of each party's perspective. Chaplains can create a bridge, allowing each side to express their concerns and beliefs openly.

> **Active Listening**: Chaplains must listen attentively to patients and families, understanding the depth and nuances of their spiritual or religious concerns. At the same time, they must be sensitive to the medical team's perspective, including the limitations of treatment options.

> **Clarifying Beliefs**: Patients or families may struggle to articulate the religious or spiritual beliefs influencing their decisions. A chaplain can help them explore these beliefs and clarify what they want, often drawing on religious texts, traditions, or personal faith practices.

> **Mediating Conversations**: In situations where medical teams and families disagree, chaplains can act as mediators,

encouraging both sides to communicate openly, respectfully, and empathetically. By acknowledging the concerns of both the family and the healthcare professionals, chaplains foster understanding and reduce conflict.

b. Respecting Patient Autonomy

Patient autonomy—the right of individuals to make decisions about their own medical care based on personal beliefs and values—is a foundational ethical principle in healthcare. However, when a patient's religious or spiritual beliefs clash with medical advice, healthcare teams may find it difficult to respect these decisions, especially if they believe the patient's choice will lead to harm or suffering.

Chaplains can help affirm patient autonomy while guiding patients and families through difficult decisions. This process involves:

Supporting Informed Decision-Making: Chaplains ensure that patients and families fully understand the medical situation, including the consequences of accepting or refusing treatment, within the context of their religious beliefs.

Providing Theological Reflection: When patients or families are unsure how to align their faith with their medical decisions, chaplains can offer theological reflection to explore how their beliefs apply to their current situation. This reflection often helps families make decisions that both honor their faith and acknowledge medical realities.

Encouraging Reconciliation Between Beliefs and Care: In some cases, patients or families may be able to find common ground that reconciles their religious beliefs with medical advice. Chaplains can facilitate this process by offering spiritual resources, such as prayer, scripture, or religious rituals, that help align their faith with the necessary medical interventions.

c. Navigating Institutional and Legal Boundaries

At times, ethical dilemmas arise because hospital policies, state laws, or professional medical guidelines restrict the choices available to patients and their families. For example, laws regarding abortion, euthanasia, or certain life-sustaining treatments may conflict with a patient's religious beliefs or preferences.

Chaplains must be aware of these boundaries while still advocating for the patient's spiritual and emotional needs. This often requires a delicate balancing act:

Educating Patients About Legal and Policy Limitations: Chaplains may need to explain hospital policies or state regulations to patients and families who are unaware of the restrictions on certain medical decisions. However, this must be done with sensitivity, offering spiritual comfort alongside the information.

Supporting Families in Accepting Unfavorable Outcomes: When medical or legal realities prevent patients from receiving the care they believe they need, chaplains can help them process these frustrations spiritually. Offering prayers, scripture, or spiritual rituals may help families cope with the difficult emotions that arise when their wishes are not honored.

3. Navigating Cultural and Religious Diversity

In today's pluralistic society, chaplains must be prepared to encounter a wide variety of religious beliefs, cultural values, and spiritual practices. Ethical dilemmas can become particularly complex in a multicultural setting, where chaplains must navigate not only the beliefs of the patient and their family but also those of the medical staff, who may come from different cultural or religious backgrounds.

Understanding Diverse Beliefs: Chaplains need to educate themselves about the spiritual beliefs and cultural practices of the diverse populations they serve. Understanding how different traditions view life, death, and medical care helps chaplains offer compassionate and respectful guidance.

Avoiding Bias: Chaplains must be vigilant against allowing their own beliefs to influence their guidance inappropriately. The goal is to support the patient's spiritual needs, not to impose the chaplain's religious views.

Creating a Spirit of Mutual Respect: When cultural or religious beliefs differ sharply between the medical staff and the patient or family, chaplains can foster an environment of mutual respect. Acknowledging the validity of each party's perspective while focusing on the shared goal of the patient's well-being can de-escalate tension.

4. Addressing Theological and Philosophical Conflicts

In an age of postmodernity, where skepticism toward religion and the existence of God is increasingly common, chaplains may face theological or philosophical conflicts. A patient or family might reject the existence of God or spiritual beliefs altogether, while others may question why a benevolent God allows suffering, especially in the context of illness and death.

Engaging with Atheism and Secularism: Chaplains can engage in compassionate dialogue with patients or families who express atheism or secular views, focusing on shared values such as human dignity, peace, and comfort in suffering. Rhetorical questions that challenge atheistic worldviews—"If there is no God, where does hope come from in moments of deep suffering?"—can open space for spiritual reflection without imposing belief.

Offering Spiritual Resources: When families struggle with theological doubts, especially concerning the problem of evil or suffering, chaplains can offer spiritual guidance that encourages deeper reflection. They might explore theological perspectives on suffering, emphasizing the mystery of faith and the possibility of finding meaning and redemption even in difficult circumstances.

Encouraging Personal Reflection: Patients and families who wrestle with theological or philosophical doubts can benefit from personal reflection guided by a chaplain. Reflecting on their life's purpose, past experiences, and spiritual journeys may help them come to terms with their situation.

Conclusion: The Chaplain's Role in Navigating Ethical Dilemmas

Navigating ethical dilemmas in healthcare requires a delicate balance of respect for patient autonomy, medical realities, spiritual beliefs, and institutional policies. Chaplains are called to stand at the crossroads of these challenges, offering compassionate support, theological reflection, and spiritual guidance that helps patients and families make informed decisions. By fostering open communication, advocating for patient needs, and engaging with both the medical and spiritual dimensions of care, chaplains provide essential guidance through the complexities of ethical healthcare decisions. Ultimately, chaplains serve as bridges between worlds—medical, spiritual, and ethical—offering a beacon of hope and understanding in the face of life's most profound challenges.

Building Relationships with Healthcare Professionals

In a healthcare environment, chaplains play a vital role as part of the interdisciplinary care team. Their ability to build strong, collaborative relationships with doctors, nurses, and other medical staff is essential to ensure that spiritual care complements medical treatment, enhancing the overall well-being of patients. While the chaplain's focus is primarily on the spiritual, emotional, and relational aspects of care, integrating their expertise into the medical team's work requires mutual respect, clear communication, and an understanding of how spiritual care supports holistic health.

This section explores the importance of fostering trust, communication, and collaboration between chaplains and healthcare professionals, highlighting practical ways to integrate spiritual care into the healthcare system.

1. The Importance of Collaborative Relationships

In modern healthcare, there is increasing recognition of the need for holistic care—treating not only the physical symptoms of illness but also the emotional, psychological, and spiritual dimensions of well-being. Spiritual care has been shown to improve patient outcomes, providing comfort, hope, and meaning in the face of illness, suffering, and uncertainty. However, for this approach to be effective, chaplains must collaborate closely with healthcare professionals to ensure that spiritual care is seen as a complement to medical treatment, not an isolated aspect of care.

a. A Unified Approach to Patient Care

When chaplains and healthcare professionals work together effectively, patients benefit from a more unified approach to care. In times of crisis, such as life-threatening illness, trauma, or end-of-life decisions, patients and families often experience intense spiritual and emotional turmoil. Doctors and nurses may focus on providing medical interventions, but without attending to the emotional and spiritual dimensions of care, patients may feel disconnected or unsupported in other critical areas of their well-being. By collaborating with chaplains, healthcare providers can offer a more comprehensive approach that addresses all aspects of the patient's experience.

b. Enhancing Patient Well-being

Studies have shown that patients who receive spiritual care report improved psychological well-being, reduced anxiety, and a greater sense of peace, particularly in palliative care and end-of-life situations. When chaplains are integrated into the healthcare team, they can provide timely spiritual interventions—such as prayers, sacraments, or counseling—that enhance the medical care provided by doctors and nurses. By being part of the team, chaplains can also help medical staff identify when a patient may be in spiritual distress, ensuring that these needs are met early in the care process.

2. Developing Mutual Trust and Respect

Building a strong relationship with healthcare professionals begins with establishing mutual trust and respect. Chaplains bring a unique set of skills and insights to the care team, but to be effective collaborators, they must demonstrate professionalism, a clear understanding of their role, and a deep respect for the expertise of the medical staff. At the same time, healthcare providers must be open to the chaplain's contributions, recognizing the value of spiritual care in improving patient outcomes.

a. Understanding the Role of Healthcare Professionals

Chaplains should take the time to understand the roles and responsibilities of healthcare professionals, appreciating the pressures they face in delivering medical care. Doctors, nurses, and other healthcare providers are often working in fast-paced, high-stress environments where life-and-death decisions must be made quickly. Chaplains must be sensitive to these demands, understanding that their role is to complement, not compete with, the work of the medical team.

b. Demonstrating Professionalism and Competence

To gain the trust of healthcare professionals, chaplains must consistently demonstrate professionalism and competence in their role. This includes being punctual, maintaining confidentiality, and adhering to the ethical guidelines of healthcare chaplaincy. Chaplains should be knowledgeable about medical terminology and the processes involved in patient care, which allows them to communicate effectively with medical staff. By demonstrating a commitment to high standards, chaplains can earn the respect of their colleagues.

c. Acknowledging Boundaries

Respecting professional boundaries is key to building trust. Chaplains must understand the limits of their role and avoid encroaching on medical responsibilities. For example, chaplains should not offer medical advice or attempt to influence medical decisions beyond providing spiritual support. By staying within the scope of their expertise, chaplains can avoid potential conflicts and foster positive working relationships.

3. Effective Communication with Healthcare Professionals

Clear, effective communication is essential for collaboration between chaplains and healthcare professionals. By maintaining open lines of communication, chaplains can ensure that the spiritual care they provide aligns with the medical care patients receive.

a. Participating in Care Team Meetings

Chaplains should actively participate in care team meetings or rounds, where healthcare professionals discuss patient progress and care plans. This allows chaplains to stay informed about the patient's medical situation and to offer insights on the spiritual or emotional needs they have observed. When chaplains contribute to these meetings, they help integrate spiritual care into the overall care strategy, ensuring a coordinated approach.

b. Providing Timely Updates on Spiritual Needs

Chaplains should communicate regularly with healthcare professionals about any spiritual concerns or needs that may impact a patient's medical treatment. For example, if a patient's religious beliefs affect their willingness to accept certain treatments (such as blood transfusions or life-sustaining interventions), the chaplain can alert the medical team and help facilitate discussions between the patient, family, and healthcare providers. Timely communication ensures that all aspects of care are considered, reducing the potential for misunderstandings or conflicts.

c. Maintaining Clear Documentation

Chaplains can document their spiritual care interventions in the patient's medical record, where appropriate, ensuring that healthcare professionals are aware of the chaplain's involvement. This documentation can include information about spiritual assessments, pastoral visits, prayers offered, or any concerns raised by the patient or family. Clear documentation helps ensure continuity of care, especially when multiple healthcare providers are involved in the patient's treatment.

4. Building Relationships Through Empathy and Understanding

In the often intense and emotionally charged environment of healthcare, chaplains can build strong relationships with medical staff by offering empathy and understanding, not just to patients, but to the staff themselves. Healthcare professionals regularly witness suffering, trauma, and loss, which can lead to compassion fatigue or burnout. Chaplains, as pastoral caregivers, are in a unique position to offer support not only to patients and families but also to healthcare professionals.

a. Providing Emotional Support to Healthcare Professionals

Doctors and nurses may be overwhelmed by the emotional demands of their work, especially in areas such as oncology, critical care, or palliative care. Chaplains can offer a listening ear, prayer, or simply a compassionate presence to help alleviate the emotional toll that healthcare workers may experience. By caring for the caregivers, chaplains contribute to the overall well-being of the healthcare team, helping them maintain resilience and avoid burnout.

b. Offering Spiritual Care to Medical Staff

In addition to emotional support, chaplains can offer spiritual care to healthcare professionals who may need guidance or comfort in their personal faith journeys. This can include leading staff prayer services, offering moments of reflection, or providing one-on-one spiritual support. Recognizing that healthcare workers also face their own spiritual struggles—especially when dealing with complex medical cases or loss—chaplains can foster a culture of compassion and healing that benefits both the staff and the patients they care for.

5. Advocating for the Integration of Spiritual Care

Chaplains play an important role in advocating for the integration of spiritual care within the healthcare system. By educating healthcare professionals about the importance of spiritual care and its impact on patient well-being, chaplains help ensure that spiritual needs are addressed as part of the patient's overall care plan. This advocacy can take several forms:

a. Educating Medical Staff on Spiritual Care

Many healthcare professionals may not fully understand the role of spiritual care in the healing process. Chaplains can offer educational workshops, in-service training, or informal discussions to explain the spiritual care process and its benefits. This helps medical staff recognize when to refer patients to the chaplain and how spiritual care can complement medical treatment.

b. Promoting a Holistic Approach to Patient Care

Chaplains can advocate for a holistic approach to care that includes physical, emotional, and spiritual well-being. This may involve working with hospital administrators or policy makers to ensure that chaplaincy services are fully integrated into patient care pathways, ensuring that all patients have access to spiritual support as part of their treatment.

Conclusion: The Power of Collaboration

Building strong relationships with healthcare professionals is essential for chaplains to provide effective spiritual care in a hospital setting. Through trust, communication, empathy, and mutual respect, chaplains can become valuable members of the healthcare team, ensuring that spiritual care is seamlessly integrated into patient treatment. By working together, chaplains and healthcare professionals can provide a holistic approach to care that addresses the physical, emotional, and spiritual needs of patients, fostering healing and hope in even the most challenging circumstances.

Conducting Bedside Prayers, Rituals, and Sacraments

In healthcare chaplaincy, one of the most profound aspects of spiritual care is offering bedside prayers, rituals, and sacraments to patients and their families. These practices serve as powerful reminders of God's presence, offer comfort in moments of suffering, and provide hope and peace in the face of illness or death. Chaplains are often called upon to perform these sacred acts, and their ability to do so with sensitivity and compassion can greatly influence the spiritual and emotional well-being of those they serve.

1. The Role of Prayer in Spiritual Comfort

Prayer is often the first and most natural way chaplains engage with patients. Whether it's an extemporaneous prayer spoken from the heart or a formal prayer from a religious tradition, prayer provides an opportunity for patients and their loved ones to connect with God in the midst of their suffering. For many, the act of praying reminds them that they are not alone in their struggle, that their pain is seen, and that they are part of something greater than their immediate circumstances.

a. Offering Personalized Prayers

Chaplains must be attentive to the spiritual needs and backgrounds of those they serve. Not all patients will belong to the same religious tradition, and some may have a very personal understanding of spirituality. When offering prayers, it is important to listen first and discern the spiritual language that will resonate most deeply with the patient and their family. Personalized prayers that speak directly to the patient's fears, hopes, and situation often bring the most comfort.

For example, a prayer might include petitions for healing, for strength to endure a painful treatment, or for peace as a patient faces the end of life. When a chaplain tailors the words of a prayer to the individual's specific needs, it reassures the patient that their spiritual well-being is taken seriously and that they are cared for deeply.

b. Praying for Peace and Comfort

In moments of crisis, such as when a patient is facing a terminal illness or the possibility of death, prayers for peace, comfort, and assurance become especially important. Chaplains can offer prayers that speak to God's comforting presence, encouraging patients to place their trust in divine providence. These prayers can also include words that help alleviate anxiety or fear, reminding patients and their families that they are held in God's care, even in moments of uncertainty.

2. Rituals and Sacraments in Hospital Ministry

Rituals and sacraments have the ability to transcend the pain and uncertainty of illness, bringing patients and their families into a sacred space of healing, reflection, and connection with the divine. Whether it's the familiar rituals of a specific faith tradition or new rituals that are meaningful in the context of healthcare ministry, these acts can provide a deep sense of comfort and spiritual grounding.

a. Administering the Sacraments

For patients who belong to sacramental traditions—such as Catholicism, Orthodoxy, or certain Protestant denominations—the sacraments play a central role in their spiritual lives, especially in times of sickness. The most commonly requested sacraments in hospitals include:

Anointing of the Sick (Last Rites): This sacrament is traditionally offered to those who are seriously ill or near death. The chaplain or priest anoints the patient with oil, invoking God's healing grace and offering prayers for peace and strength. This sacred ritual is a reminder of God's love and mercy, bringing comfort to both the patient and their family.

Holy Communion (Eucharist): For many Christian patients, receiving the Eucharist while in the hospital can be a profound source of spiritual nourishment. The chaplain administers the bread and wine (or grape juice, as appropriate), symbolizing the presence of Christ and reinforcing the patient's connection to their faith community, even in the midst of physical separation due to illness.

Confession (Reconciliation): In moments of illness, patients may feel the need to confess sins and seek reconciliation with God. Chaplains may be called upon to listen to confessions and offer words of absolution, helping the patient experience spiritual cleansing and renewal. This act of reconciliation often brings profound peace, especially for patients nearing the end of life.

b. Creating Meaningful Rituals

Not all patients will belong to a sacramental tradition, but the use of ritual is still important for providing spiritual comfort and structure. Chaplains can create or adapt rituals to meet the needs of patients from different religious backgrounds or those who are spiritual but not religious. These rituals can involve elements such as:

- **Lighting candles** to symbolize hope or prayer.
- **Offering blessings** to mark important transitions, such as the beginning of a difficult treatment or the acceptance of a diagnosis.
- **Reading sacred texts or poems** that bring comfort and reflection.
- **Symbolic acts** like the washing of hands, which can represent the release of fear, guilt, or pain.

These acts, while simple, can carry great spiritual weight and help patients and families process their experiences in a sacred context.

3. Sensitivity to the Needs of the Patient and Family

When conducting prayers, rituals, or sacraments at the bedside, chaplains must be deeply sensitive to the patient's condition, their spiritual background, and the emotional atmosphere in the room. A chaplain's role is to meet people where they are, offering support without imposing a specific agenda or set of beliefs.

a. Respecting Diverse Faith Traditions

In diverse healthcare settings, patients and families may come from a wide variety of religious or spiritual traditions. Chaplains must be flexible and well-versed in interfaith ministry, understanding the key rituals and prayers from different faiths. When serving patients of other religions, chaplains can offer prayers and rituals that honor the patient's spiritual journey, even if the chaplain does not share that specific faith tradition.

For example, a chaplain may offer prayers using universal language that invokes God's love and healing without referencing a particular theological framework. Additionally, chaplains should be aware of any sacred objects or rituals that are important to the patient, such as placing a rosary near the patient's bed, offering prayers in the direction of Mecca for Muslim patients, or creating a sacred space for meditation.

b. Being Attuned to Emotional Dynamics

In healthcare settings, the emotional dynamics in the room can be complex. Patients may be struggling with fear, grief, anger, or confusion, and their families may be feeling similarly overwhelmed. Chaplains need to be attuned to these dynamics and adjust their approach accordingly. Some situations may call for quiet, contemplative prayer, while others may need words of assurance and encouragement. The chaplain must also be sensitive to the pacing and duration of rituals, ensuring they do not overwhelm patients or families who are already emotionally and physically fatigued.

4. The Power of Presence in Rituals

While prayers and sacraments provide structure and meaning, the chaplain's presence is often the most important aspect of the ritual. Simply being there—offering a listening ear, holding a patient's hand, or sitting in silent prayer—can bring immense comfort. The chaplain's presence communicates care, concern, and God's love in tangible ways.

a. The Ministry of Presence

The ministry of presence refers to the chaplain's ability to be fully present with the patient and their family, offering emotional and spiritual support without necessarily saying or doing anything. This presence can turn ordinary moments into sacred encounters, as the chaplain holds space for the patient's experience of suffering, fear, or hope. This practice, especially during bedside rituals, creates an environment where God's grace and peace can be felt, even in the midst of great pain.

b. Silent Prayer and Reflection

There are times when words fail, and silent prayer or reflection becomes the most powerful form of ministry. Sitting quietly with a patient who is too weak to speak, or offering silent prayers for a family awaiting difficult news, allows the chaplain to be fully present in the moment. This silent accompaniment demonstrates that spiritual support is not always about words, but about the shared experience of compassion, love, and connection.

Conclusion: Bringing Spiritual Comfort to Those in Need

Conducting bedside prayers, rituals, and sacraments is a deeply sacred task that allows chaplains to bring spiritual comfort to patients and families during some of life's most difficult moments. By offering personalized prayers, administering sacraments, creating meaningful rituals, and being fully present, chaplains provide a sense of peace, hope, and divine presence in the midst of suffering. These spiritual practices, conducted with sensitivity and care, remind patients that they are not alone—that they are held in the care of a loving God, even in their darkest hours.

CHAPTER 5

Universal Human Needs in Chaplaincy

Recognizing the Universality of Human Needs: Spiritual, Emotional, and Physical

Chaplains must understand that the core needs of humanity—spiritual, emotional, and physical—are universal. These needs transcend cultural, religious, and personal differences, reflecting the common experiences shared by all people regardless of background. As a chaplain, one must be attuned to these shared aspects of human existence to provide holistic care, whether in prisons, hospitals, or other settings. In this chapter, we will explore how chaplains can minister effectively by recognizing and addressing the universal nature of these needs.

1. Spiritual Needs: The Search for Meaning and Connection

At the core of every human being lies a profound spiritual longing—a desire for meaning, connection, and a sense of purpose. This search is a fundamental aspect of human existence and is not limited to any one religion, culture, or belief system. It is the inner drive that propels individuals to make sense of their lives, especially in moments of crisis, vulnerability, or suffering. Whether one identifies as religious, spiritual, or secular, the need for purpose and connection transcends all boundaries.

In times of personal crisis—such as illness, imprisonment, or the loss of a loved one—this spiritual need often comes to the forefront. Faced with their own mortality, deep suffering, or the guilt of past actions, individuals begin to question the meaning of their lives and the events that have led them to their current state. These moments, though challenging, provide unique opportunities for chaplains to offer guidance, comfort, and spiritual support.

The Crisis of Meaning in Times of Suffering

Suffering, whether physical, emotional, or spiritual, naturally raises questions of meaning. In hospitals, for example, a patient facing a terminal illness may ask, "Why me?" or "What is the purpose of this suffering?" Similarly, inmates in prisons may grapple with questions like, "Am I beyond redemption?" or "How can I find meaning after all the wrong I've done?" These are not simple questions, and they often come with deep emotional and psychological turmoil. In these moments, chaplains are called to walk alongside individuals as they wrestle with these spiritual challenges.

Suffering can be a catalyst for individuals to seek a deeper understanding of their lives, their relationships, and their place in the world. When illness strikes or freedom is taken away, the structures that gave a sense of identity, security, and control are often shattered. This leads many to search for a new sense of purpose or meaning—one that can accommodate the reality of pain and suffering.

For some, this process may lead them to reconnect with their faith or explore spiritual practices for the first time. Others may find meaning in their relationships, in acts of service, or in the legacy they will leave behind. The chaplain's role is not necessarily to provide definitive answers to these questions, but rather to create a space where individuals can explore their own answers, offering guidance and support along the way.

Connection to the Divine or the Sacred

Another central aspect of spiritual care is the desire for connection—particularly a connection with the Divine or with something greater than oneself. For many people, this connection is experienced through prayer, meditation, or religious rituals. These practices offer a sense of comfort and reassurance, reminding individuals that they are not alone in their suffering and that there is a higher power at work in their lives.

In moments of crisis, individuals often turn to their faith as a source of strength and hope. Patients may request prayers or religious rites, while inmates may seek spiritual counsel to reconnect with God. For people of faith, this connection with the Divine can provide a deep sense of peace, even in the face of profound suffering or uncertainty.

However, not all individuals have a clear or established connection with a specific religious tradition. Some may identify as spiritual but not religious, while others may not believe in a higher power at all. Yet, even in these cases, the longing for connection remains. Chaplains must be prepared to help individuals explore this need for connection in whatever way is most meaningful to them—whether that is through a relationship with God, a connection to the universe, or a sense of oneness with humanity.

Finding Purpose in Suffering

One of the most difficult yet important spiritual tasks is finding purpose in suffering. Illness, incarceration, or personal loss can often feel meaningless, leaving individuals feeling hopeless and adrift. Chaplains are uniquely positioned to help individuals reframe their suffering, allowing them to see it not as an obstacle but as an opportunity for growth, transformation, and even healing.

In religious contexts, suffering is often viewed as part of the human experience, a way to connect with the suffering of Christ or as a test of faith. For Christians, for example, the Bible offers many stories of individuals who found meaning in their suffering—stories that can serve as sources of hope for those currently experiencing pain. The story of Job, who endured immense suffering yet remained faithful to God, or the Apostle Paul, who wrote letters of encouragement while imprisoned, are powerful reminders of the possibility of finding purpose even in hardship.

For those without a particular religious framework, chaplains can help them reflect on how their suffering might contribute to their personal growth or the greater good. For example, someone facing a terminal illness may find purpose in mending broken relationships, passing on wisdom to loved ones, or helping others through similar situations. Inmates may come to see their time in prison as an opportunity for self-reflection, personal growth, or spiritual awakening.

The Chaplain's Role in Spiritual Care

As a chaplain, offering spiritual care means helping individuals explore these questions of meaning and connection in a compassionate and non-judgmental way. This often involves active listening, providing a safe space for individuals to express their fears, doubts, and spiritual struggles. Rather than offering quick solutions or platitudes, chaplains walk alongside individuals as they navigate these difficult journeys, providing comfort and support when needed.

Chaplains also serve as spiritual guides, helping individuals reconnect with their faith or explore new spiritual practices that may bring them comfort. For people of faith, this may involve offering prayers, reading from sacred texts, or performing religious rituals. For others, it may involve offering opportunities for meditation, reflection, or simply being present in silence.

The chaplain's goal is not to impose their own beliefs or answers but to support individuals in discovering their own spiritual resources. Whether through prayer, conversation, or quiet reflection, chaplains offer a sense of hope and meaning that can be profoundly transformative, especially in moments of crisis.

Conclusion: A Shared Human Longing

The search for meaning and connection is a universal aspect of the human experience. In times of suffering, illness, or incarceration, this need becomes even more pronounced, as individuals grapple with questions about their purpose, their faith, and their place in the world. As chaplains, we are called to accompany individuals on this spiritual journey, offering guidance, comfort, and a sense of hope. By recognizing and honoring this shared human longing, we can provide meaningful and transformative care, helping individuals find peace and purpose in the midst of life's most difficult challenges.

a. The Need for Purpose and Hope

In both hospital and prison settings, individuals often find themselves grappling with profound existential questions—questions about their purpose, their worth, and the meaning behind their suffering. For patients facing life-threatening illnesses, questions like "Why is this happening to me?" or "What is the meaning of my pain?" arise as they confront their own mortality. Similarly, inmates, weighed down by guilt and shame from their past actions, often struggle to find redemption and a renewed sense of purpose. In both cases, there is a deep need for something beyond immediate relief—a need for purpose and hope that transcends their current circumstances.

As chaplains, we are called to enter into these moments of spiritual crisis, to sit with individuals in their pain and uncertainty, and to help them seek and discover meaning. It is not just about providing theological answers but also about offering the comfort of God's presence and the promise of hope—a hope that looks toward tomorrow, a hope that reminds them that their lives still hold value and potential, even in the midst of hardship.

The Crisis of Purpose in Suffering

When life is interrupted by illness or incarceration, it can feel as though all sense of purpose has been stripped away. In a hospital, a once-active individual may find themselves suddenly dependent on others, unable to contribute to the world in the way they once did. For an inmate, the isolation and confinement of prison can magnify feelings of failure, helplessness, or abandonment. These experiences can lead individuals to question their worth: "What is my purpose now?" or "What good can come from my suffering?"

This crisis of purpose often stems from the loss of control and identity that illness or imprisonment brings. When people can no longer rely on their bodies, their freedom, or their routines, they are forced to confront deeper questions about what gives their life meaning beyond the circumstances they find themselves in. This is where chaplains play a crucial role—by gently guiding people to explore new ways of understanding their purpose, even in the midst of difficulty.

The Search for Redemption and Renewal

In prison settings, the need for purpose is often intertwined with a longing for redemption. Inmates may feel burdened by their past actions, weighed down by guilt and shame. They may struggle to believe that they can ever be forgiven or that their lives have any worth after what they have done. The chaplain's role here is to help inmates navigate these heavy emotions and to remind them that redemption and renewal are possible.

Through spiritual guidance and pastoral care, chaplains can help inmates see their worth beyond their crimes, encouraging them to seek forgiveness from others, from themselves, and from God. This journey is not easy, but it is one filled with hope—hope that through reconciliation and spiritual growth, inmates can rebuild their lives and find a renewed sense of purpose. Whether through faith, personal reflection, or acts of service within the prison community, inmates can begin to reclaim their sense of worth and look toward a future beyond the walls of the prison.

Offering Hope to the Suffering

For patients in a hospital, especially those dealing with chronic illness or terminal diagnoses, the need for hope can be equally urgent. Suffering can feel all-consuming, overshadowing any sense of meaning or hope for the future. As a result, patients may experience deep despair, feeling that their lives no longer have value or purpose. Chaplains, in these moments, become vessels of hope, reminding patients that their lives still have meaning and that their suffering does not define their worth.

The hope chaplains offer may come in many forms. For people of faith, it may be a reminder of God's promises, the hope of eternal life, or the belief that their suffering has a higher purpose. For those who do not identify with a specific religious tradition, hope may come in the form of finding peace in their relationships, recognizing the love and care they still have to offer, or discovering inner strength that helps them endure. In either case, chaplains help individuals hold onto hope, even when their bodies are failing or their future feels uncertain.

The Chaplain's Role in Nurturing Hope

The work of a chaplain is ultimately a ministry of hope. We are called to help individuals tap into the spiritual resources available to them—whether that is through faith in God, a sense of connection to humanity, or personal resilience. We walk alongside people as they wrestle with their suffering, offering them a space to voice their fears and doubts, and encouraging them to see that, even in their darkest moments, hope is still possible.

This need for meaning and hope is not limited to religious individuals. Even those who do not subscribe to a particular faith tradition often search for a framework that helps them make sense of their experiences and find peace. The chaplain's role, therefore, is not to impose religious answers but to help individuals draw on whatever spiritual resources are available to them. This could mean offering prayers and sacraments to a Christian patient, providing spiritual companionship to someone exploring new beliefs, or simply being a non-judgmental presence for a patient or inmate who feels lost.

Chaplains offer more than just comfort; they offer a vision of a future filled with hope—a future in which suffering does not have the final word. By helping individuals find purpose in their pain and suffering, and by pointing them toward the possibility of healing and renewal, chaplains serve as both guides and companions on the journey toward hope. Through prayer, listening, and compassionate presence, we help people rediscover their sense of worth and purpose, even in the most difficult of circumstances.

Conclusion: A Ministry of Purpose and Hope

At the heart of chaplaincy is the recognition that every person, no matter their circumstances, needs a sense of purpose and hope. In both hospitals and prisons, individuals are often confronted with experiences that shake the very foundations of their identity and sense of self. As chaplains, we are called to offer comfort and guidance in these moments of crisis, reminding those we serve that their lives still have value, that redemption is possible, and that there is always hope for tomorrow.

Through this ministry of presence and compassion, we help individuals rediscover their purpose, even in the midst of illness, guilt, or suffering. Whether through faith in God or a renewed connection to humanity, chaplains play a vital role in nurturing the seeds of hope that can grow and flourish, no matter the soil in which they are planted. It is this hope that brings healing, restores dignity, and provides the strength to face another day.

b. Connection with the Divine or the Sacred

Another critical aspect of spiritual care is fostering a connection with the Divine or with what the individual considers sacred. For people of faith, this connection might involve prayer, sacraments, or rituals that help them feel closer to God. For others, it may involve creating space for meditation, quiet reflection, or time spent in nature. The chaplain's task is to help people reconnect with whatever they view as transcendent, offering a sense of peace and reassurance in times of hardship.

2. Emotional Needs: The Desire for Understanding and Compassion

Emotional needs are equally universal. Every human being desires to be seen, understood, and cared for, especially during times of vulnerability. When people experience trauma, loss, or isolation, they need emotional support to process these experiences and find healing. As a chaplain, providing this emotional care is essential to fostering a sense of peace and well-being.

a. The Power of Empathy and Presence

The most profound gift chaplains offer is the ministry of presence—the simple act of being with someone in their suffering. In a world that often rushes past pain and ignores suffering, the chaplain is called to slow down and be fully present with those who are hurting. Whether it's listening to a patient process their fear of death or sitting with an inmate as they recount their guilt, the act of offering empathy and understanding can be transformative.

Empathy allows chaplains to connect with others on a deep emotional level, demonstrating that they are not alone in their pain. This is especially critical in settings like hospitals and prisons, where people often feel isolated or forgotten. By offering emotional support, chaplains affirm the inherent dignity of each individual, reminding them that they are seen, valued, and cared for, regardless of their circumstances.

b. Offering Compassionate Care Without Judgment

Emotional care also involves offering compassion without judgment. Chaplains often encounter people who are at their lowest points—patients facing terminal illness, inmates struggling with the weight of their past actions, or families grieving the loss of a loved one. In these moments, individuals may feel ashamed, guilty, or angry, and they may be hesitant to open up about their feelings. The chaplain's role is to provide a safe, non-judgmental space where these emotions can be expressed freely.

By offering compassionate care, chaplains help people process difficult emotions, facilitating healing and growth. Whether through active listening, gentle encouragement, or simply sitting in silence with someone who is grieving, the chaplain acts as a conduit for emotional healing, helping individuals move forward with a greater sense of peace.

3. Physical Needs: The Reality of Human Frailty and Suffering

Physical needs, too, are universal. Illness, pain, and suffering are part of the human condition, and everyone, at some point in life, must confront their own physical limitations. In both hospitals and prisons, chaplains encounter individuals whose physical well-being is compromised, and this physical suffering often triggers deeper spiritual and emotional crises.

a. Ministering to the Sick and Suffering

In healthcare settings, chaplains are regularly called to minister to those who are physically suffering, whether from illness, injury, or the effects of aging. This ministry often involves offering prayers for healing, but it also requires addressing the deeper spiritual and emotional concerns that arise from physical pain. Patients may be grappling with questions about the purpose of their suffering, fears about death, or anger at God or the world for their condition.

Chaplains must approach this ministry with sensitivity, recognizing that physical suffering can be a gateway to profound spiritual and emotional crises. By acknowledging the reality of pain and offering spiritual care that addresses the whole person—body, mind, and spirit—chaplains can help individuals find peace even in the midst of physical frailty.

b. Attending to the Practical Physical Needs

While chaplains are primarily responsible for spiritual care, they should also be aware of the practical physical needs of those they serve. In both hospitals and prisons, people may require basic comforts—a glass of water, a blanket, or help adjusting their position in bed. Attending to these simple needs, when possible, reinforces the chaplain's care for the whole person.

In prison settings, where physical deprivation and discomfort may be part of the daily experience, chaplains can advocate for better treatment or ensure that inmates have access to basic necessities. While chaplains may not be able to resolve all physical issues, their willingness to attend to them speaks volumes about their commitment to holistic care.

4. Common Human Experiences: Suffering, Longing, and the Desire for Healing

Regardless of background, culture, or faith, all people share certain common human experiences. Suffering is one of the most universal aspects of the human condition. Whether due to illness, imprisonment, loss, or trauma, suffering brings people to the brink of their physical, emotional, and spiritual capacities. In these moments, they long for relief, for healing, and for hope.

a. Suffering and Spiritual Growth

While suffering is painful, it is also an opportunity for spiritual growth. Chaplains can help individuals frame their suffering in a way that fosters healing and growth. For people of faith, this might involve seeing suffering as a way to participate in the suffering of Christ or as a test of faith. For others, it may be an opportunity to reflect on life's deeper meanings or to reconcile with loved ones.

In all cases, the chaplain's role is to offer guidance and support as individuals navigate their suffering, helping them find meaning and purpose in the midst of their pain.

b. The Universal Longing for Healing and Wholeness

Whether in a hospital or a prison, people desire healing—whether physical, emotional, or spiritual. This desire for healing is universal, and chaplains are uniquely positioned to help meet this need. While not all healing will be physical, chaplains can offer spiritual and emotional healing by helping individuals come to terms with their suffering, seek reconciliation with others, and find peace within themselves.

In doing so, chaplains remind those they serve that healing is not just about the absence of illness or suffering, but about achieving a sense of wholeness and peace, regardless of life's circumstances.

Conclusion: Ministering to the Whole Person

Recognizing the universality of human needs—spiritual, emotional, and physical—enables chaplains to minister effectively to people from all walks of life. Whether serving in prisons, hospitals, or other settings, chaplains are called to meet individuals in their shared experiences of suffering, longing, and the desire for healing. By addressing these needs holistically, chaplains offer comfort, hope, and spiritual support that transcends religious, cultural, and personal differences, affirming the shared humanity of all people.

CHAPTER 6

Restorative and Rehabilitative Ministry

Chaplains play a critical role in both restorative and rehabilitative ministry, particularly in prisons and hospitals where brokenness is often the defining experience of those they serve. In these challenging environments, individuals may feel lost, abandoned, or overwhelmed by their circumstances, and it is in these moments that the chaplain's ministry becomes a beacon of hope. This chapter explores how chaplains can foster healing, reconciliation, and transformation through their work, addressing the spiritual, emotional, and psychological needs of those in their care.

The Role of Restorative Ministry

Restorative ministry is a transformative process that focuses on healing the wounds of the past, providing individuals with the opportunity to confront their pain and seek a path toward reconciliation and wholeness. For chaplains serving in prisons and hospitals, this ministry plays a crucial role in facilitating healing on multiple levels—spiritual, emotional, and relational. Through restorative ministry, chaplains guide individuals as they navigate their personal journeys of healing, helping them find hope and meaning amid their struggles.

Confronting Guilt and Seeking Forgiveness

One of the most significant aspects of restorative ministry is addressing the burden of guilt that many individuals carry, especially in prison settings. For inmates, the weight of past actions can lead to feelings of shame, despair, and hopelessness. The role of the chaplain is to create a safe and supportive environment where inmates can openly confront their guilt and explore the concept of forgiveness.

1. Facilitating Self-Reflection

Chaplains encourage inmates to engage in self-reflection, guiding them through a process of examining their past actions and the impact those actions have had on themselves and others. This reflective process may involve journaling, prayer, or guided discussions. By confronting their past, inmates can begin to understand the roots of their behavior and the emotions associated with it.

2. Understanding the Nature of Forgiveness

Chaplains can provide insights into the nature of forgiveness, both in a theological context and a personal one. They emphasize that forgiveness is not about excusing wrongdoing but about freeing oneself from the shackles of guilt and shame. By exploring various theological perspectives on forgiveness, chaplains can help individuals understand the importance of seeking forgiveness not only from others but also from themselves and God.

3. Creating Opportunities for Dialogue

In some cases, chaplains can facilitate dialogues between inmates and their victims or family members, when appropriate. This restorative justice approach allows for honest conversations that can lead to mutual understanding and healing. By providing a platform for individuals to express remorse and seek forgiveness, chaplains help to mend the broken relationships that often contribute to feelings of guilt.

Making Peace with God, Family, and Oneself

In hospital settings, patients often face their own set of challenges as they grapple with terminal illnesses, serious diagnoses, or the implications of long-term health issues. Many patients find themselves seeking peace in various forms—whether it's reconciling with family members, making amends with God, or coming to terms with their own mortality.

1. Guiding Spiritual Exploration

Chaplains play a vital role in helping patients navigate their spiritual questions and struggles. This may involve facilitating discussions about faith, God, and the meaning of suffering. For patients who identify as religious, chaplains can provide spiritual rituals, prayers, and sacramental moments that foster a sense of connection to the Divine.

2. Encouraging Family Conversations

Family dynamics often shift dramatically in times of health crises. Chaplains can help facilitate conversations among family members, promoting healing and understanding. They may encourage patients and their families to express their feelings, share unresolved issues, and seek reconciliation. This process can provide a sense of closure and healing for both patients and their loved ones.

3. Promoting Self-Compassion

Many patients struggle with feelings of guilt or regret related to their health or life choices. Chaplains can guide individuals toward self-compassion, helping them to recognize that everyone makes mistakes and that forgiveness is essential for healing. By encouraging patients to treat themselves with kindness and understanding, chaplains help foster a positive self-image and encourage personal growth.

A Holistic Approach to Restoration

Restorative ministry requires a holistic approach, addressing the spiritual, emotional, and relational dimensions of healing. Chaplains must be attentive to the individual needs of those they serve, recognizing that each person's journey is unique.

1. Incorporating Various Spiritual Practices

Chaplains can draw from a variety of spiritual practices and traditions to support restorative ministry. This may include prayer, meditation, reflective writing, and participation in communal rituals. By offering diverse avenues for spiritual expression, chaplains can help individuals connect with their spiritual resources in meaningful ways.

2. Collaborating with Mental Health Professionals

Chaplains can enhance their restorative ministry by collaborating with mental health professionals. This interdisciplinary approach allows for comprehensive care, addressing both the spiritual and psychological needs of individuals. By working together, chaplains and therapists can create a more supportive environment for healing.

3. Creating a Safe and Supportive Environment

A crucial element of restorative ministry is establishing a safe space for individuals to explore their pain, share their stories, and seek healing. Chaplains must be empathetic listeners, providing a non-judgmental presence that encourages openness and vulnerability. This supportive environment fosters trust, allowing individuals to engage more deeply in the healing process.

Conclusion: The Transformative Power of Restorative Ministry

The role of restorative ministry is vital in helping individuals navigate their paths toward healing and reconciliation. By addressing issues of guilt, forgiveness, and personal peace, chaplains provide essential support to those in prisons and hospitals. Through self-reflection, dialogue, and spiritual exploration, individuals can find the healing they seek, ultimately reclaiming their sense of purpose and connection.

Restorative ministry is a testament to the transformative power of compassion, empathy, and spiritual care. It highlights the importance of meeting individuals where they are, guiding them through their struggles, and helping them rediscover hope, healing, and wholeness in their lives.

Rehabilitative Ministry in Prisons

Rehabilitative ministry in prisons is a vital aspect of chaplaincy, focusing on transforming lives and equipping inmates with the spiritual and emotional tools they need to reintegrate into society successfully. While restorative ministry addresses healing from past wounds, rehabilitative ministry emphasizes the practical steps toward personal growth, self-discovery, and the development of a renewed sense of identity. For chaplains, this means actively engaging with inmates, fostering hope, and guiding them toward meaningful change.

Breaking the Cycle of Crime and Addiction

Many inmates find themselves trapped in cycles of crime and addiction, often stemming from deeper issues such as trauma, mental health struggles, and lack of community support. Chaplains play a crucial role in addressing these underlying factors, providing spiritual mentorship and guidance that encourages inmates to confront their past behaviors and make conscious choices toward change.

1. Identifying Underlying Issues

Chaplains can help inmates identify the root causes of their criminal behavior or addiction, facilitating discussions that encourage self-awareness and reflection. By addressing these issues in a supportive environment, chaplains empower inmates to take responsibility for their actions and begin the healing process.

2. Encouraging Personal Responsibility

A key component of rehabilitative ministry is instilling a sense of personal responsibility. Chaplains encourage inmates to recognize that change is possible, but it requires effort and commitment. This may involve setting personal goals, developing coping strategies, and actively participating in rehabilitation programs. By fostering accountability, chaplains help inmates embrace the journey of transformation.

3. Creating Support Networks

Rehabilitation often thrives in community settings. Chaplains can facilitate the creation of support networks among inmates, encouraging them to lean on one another for encouragement and accountability. This sense of community can be invaluable, providing inmates with a sense of belonging and support that extends beyond their time in prison.

Spiritual Mentorship and Guidance

Chaplains serve as spiritual mentors to inmates, offering guidance and support as they navigate their rehabilitation journeys. This mentorship can take various forms, including one-on-one counseling, group sessions, and structured Bible studies.

1. Spiritual Counseling

Through spiritual counseling, chaplains provide inmates with a safe space to explore their faith, doubts, and spiritual questions. This guidance helps inmates develop a deeper understanding of their beliefs and how they relate to their experiences. Chaplains encourage inmates to view their spiritual journey as integral to their rehabilitation, helping them discover a renewed sense of purpose and direction.

2. Bible Studies and Educational Programs

Engaging inmates in Bible studies and educational programs can significantly impact their rehabilitation. Chaplains can facilitate discussions around scriptural teachings that emphasize forgiveness, redemption, and personal transformation. By exploring these themes, inmates can develop a deeper understanding of their faith and how it can inform their actions moving forward.

3. Skill-Building Workshops

In addition to spiritual growth, chaplains can offer skill-building workshops that equip inmates with practical tools for their future. This may include vocational training, life skills development, and programs focusing on conflict resolution and emotional regulation. By empowering inmates with new skills, chaplains help them envision a life beyond incarceration.

Fostering Hope and Future Vision

Hope is a powerful motivator for change. Inmates often struggle with feelings of hopelessness, believing that their past defines their future. Chaplains play a pivotal role in fostering hope, encouraging inmates to envision a new life post-incarceration.

1. Visioning Exercises

Chaplains can lead visioning exercises that help inmates articulate their hopes and dreams for the future. This process encourages inmates to think beyond their current circumstances, allowing them to create a mental image of what they want their lives to look like after release. By articulating these aspirations, inmates can develop a greater sense of agency over their lives.

2. Affirming Personal Identity

Chaplains emphasize the importance of personal identity in the rehabilitation process. Many inmates grapple with feelings of shame and worthlessness due to their past actions. Chaplains can affirm their inherent worth as individuals created in the image of God, helping them reclaim their identities and view themselves as valuable members of society.

3. Inspiring Stories of Transformation

Sharing stories of successful rehabilitation can inspire hope and motivation among inmates. Chaplains can introduce them to testimonies of individuals who have faced similar struggles but have successfully transformed their lives. These narratives serve as powerful reminders that change is possible and that a brighter future awaits them.

Preparing for Reintegration

A crucial aspect of rehabilitative ministry is preparing inmates for reintegration into society. This involves helping them develop a realistic understanding of the challenges they may face after release and providing them with the support they need to navigate this transition successfully.

1. Life Skills Training

Chaplains can facilitate life skills training that addresses practical needs such as job readiness, financial literacy, and communication skills. By equipping inmates with these tools, chaplains help ensure that they are better prepared to face the demands of life outside prison.

2. Community Connections

Building connections with local community resources is essential for successful reintegration. Chaplains can help inmates identify support services such as housing assistance, job placement programs, and counseling resources. By connecting inmates with these services, chaplains enhance their chances of successful reentry into society.

3. Ongoing Support and Mentorship

Reintegration does not end with release; it is an ongoing process. Chaplains can offer continued support and mentorship, helping inmates navigate the complexities of life outside prison walls. This ongoing relationship can be instrumental in preventing recidivism and fostering lasting change.

Conclusion: The Transformative Power of Rehabilitative Ministry

Rehabilitative ministry in prisons is a vital component of the chaplain's role, focusing on the holistic transformation of individuals seeking a new path in life. By addressing the root causes of criminal behavior, fostering hope, and preparing inmates for reintegration, chaplains play a crucial role in breaking cycles of crime and addiction.

Through spiritual mentorship, educational programs, and life skills training, chaplains empower inmates to embrace their identities as valuable members of society. Ultimately, rehabilitative ministry highlights the possibility of change and redemption, offering a pathway toward healing, purpose, and a brighter future.

The Power of Reconciliation

The Power of Reconciliation

Reconciliation stands at the heart of both restorative and rehabilitative ministry, serving as a bridge between past transgressions and future hope. It encompasses the process of healing broken relationships—be it with God, oneself, or others. For chaplains, fostering reconciliation is not merely an important task; it is a profound spiritual journey that can lead to transformative change in the lives of those they serve. This section explores practical ways in which chaplains can help individuals seek and find reconciliation, especially within the challenging context of prison ministry.

1. Reconciliation with God

Reconciliation with God is often the first step for inmates on the path to healing. Many incarcerated individuals grapple with feelings of abandonment, guilt, and shame, making it crucial for chaplains to guide them in restoring their relationship with the Divine.

a. Spiritual Counseling

Chaplains can provide spiritual counseling sessions that create a safe space for inmates to express their feelings about God and their spiritual struggles. These sessions may involve:

Confession and Repentance: Encouraging inmates to confront their sins and seek forgiveness through prayer and spiritual reflection. Chaplains can lead them through the process of acknowledging their wrongdoings and understanding God's grace.

Scriptural Guidance: Utilizing relevant biblical passages that speak to forgiveness, mercy, and reconciliation. By helping inmates connect scriptural truths to their lives, chaplains can offer hope and assurance of God's love.

Prayer Practices: Assisting inmates in developing personal prayer practices that foster intimacy with God. These practices can help them feel connected to the Divine, even in the isolation of prison.

b. Group Worship and Support

Group worship services can also play a vital role in fostering reconciliation with God. Chaplains can organize worship sessions where inmates can collectively express their faith, share their struggles, and seek forgiveness together. The power of community support in these spiritual moments can reinforce their commitment to healing and transformation.

2. Reconciliation with Oneself

For many inmates, reconciling with oneself is often the most challenging aspect of the healing process. Incarceration brings about deep self-reflection, and feelings of regret, shame, and unworthiness can hinder personal growth. Chaplains can assist inmates in this reconciliation journey by focusing on self-acceptance and personal responsibility.

a. Facilitating Self-Reflection

Chaplains can guide inmates in exploring their inner thoughts and feelings through reflective practices such as journaling or guided meditation. These practices encourage inmates to confront their past actions, acknowledge their pain, and begin the process of self-forgiveness.

b. Promoting Positive Identity Formation

Chaplains can help inmates redefine their identities beyond their past mistakes. By emphasizing their worth as individuals created in the image of God, chaplains can instill a sense of dignity and value. This may involve:

Affirmations: Encouraging inmates to develop personal affirmations that reinforce their positive qualities and potential for change.

Skill Development: Helping inmates identify and cultivate their strengths through educational programs, vocational training, and spiritual growth initiatives. By focusing on their abilities, chaplains foster a renewed sense of purpose and self-worth.

3. Reconciliation with Others

Reconciliation with others is often the most complex aspect of the healing journey. Inmates may have strained relationships with family members, victims, or peers. Chaplains play a vital role in facilitating this process, helping individuals navigate conflicts and seek forgiveness.

a. Mediation and Conflict Resolution

Chaplains can serve as mediators in conflicts between inmates and their families or victims. This may involve:

Family Counseling: Organizing family visits where inmates can engage in structured conversations with their loved ones. Chaplains can facilitate these discussions, promoting openness, honesty, and the sharing of feelings.

Restorative Justice Programs: Implementing restorative justice initiatives that allow inmates to meet with victims in a safe environment. These programs can help inmates take responsibility for their actions, listen to the impact of their behavior, and offer genuine apologies. Such encounters foster healing for both parties.

b. Encouraging Forgiveness

Chaplains can emphasize the importance of forgiveness in the reconciliation process. They can guide inmates in understanding that forgiveness is a gift they give themselves as much as it is for others. By encouraging inmates to release feelings of anger and resentment, chaplains can help them find emotional and spiritual freedom.

4. The Transformative Impact of Reconciliation

The process of reconciliation is not only healing for the individual; it can also have a transformative impact on the entire community. When inmates experience reconciliation with God, themselves, and others, they are more likely to emerge as individuals committed to positive change.

a. Restoring Relationships

Reconciliation fosters the restoration of relationships, both within the prison environment and in the broader community. As inmates mend ties with family members and victims, they contribute to a cycle of healing that extends beyond their own lives.

b. Promoting Peace and Harmony

A reconciled individual is often more equipped to contribute to a peaceful environment. As chaplains facilitate reconciliation processes, they promote a culture of understanding and forgiveness, leading to improved relationships among inmates and staff.

c. Encouraging Positive Community Engagement

Finally, individuals who experience the power of reconciliation are more likely to engage positively with their communities upon release. They carry with them the lessons learned through the reconciliation process, leading to healthier relationships and a commitment to making amends for past actions.

Conclusion: The Lifelong Journey of Reconciliation

The power of reconciliation cannot be overstated in the context of prison ministry. Chaplains play a crucial role in guiding individuals through the multifaceted journey of reconciling with God, themselves, and others. By providing spiritual guidance, facilitating conversations, and promoting forgiveness, chaplains help inmates experience profound transformation and healing.

Ultimately, reconciliation is a lifelong journey, extending beyond prison walls and into the hearts of those seeking wholeness. As chaplains continue to foster reconciliation, they contribute to building a more compassionate society, where individuals are empowered to embrace their identities and actively pursue peace and healing.

CHAPTER 7

Confidentiality in Chaplaincy

Confidentiality is a cornerstone of chaplaincy work, underpinning the trust that forms the basis of effective spiritual care. It is an ethical imperative that allows chaplains to fulfill their roles with integrity, compassion, and respect. This chapter delves into the significance of confidentiality in chaplaincy, focusing on its ethical standards, the challenges faced in both prison and hospital settings, and the balance between confidentiality and advocacy.

Ethical Standards of Confidentiality

1. The Moral and Spiritual Responsibility

Maintaining confidentiality is not merely a legal requirement; it is a moral and spiritual responsibility that chaplains must uphold. Chaplains are entrusted with sensitive information regarding individuals' spiritual struggles, personal histories, and medical conditions. This trust must never be broken lightly, as it can have profound implications for the individuals involved.

Confidentiality is grounded in the following ethical principles:

Trust: Confidentiality fosters a safe space for individuals to express their fears, doubts, and vulnerabilities. When chaplains assure those they serve that their conversations will remain confidential, it establishes a foundation of trust that is essential for effective ministry.

Dignity: Every person has the right to privacy. By respecting confidentiality, chaplains honor the dignity of individuals and validate their right to control their personal narratives.

Spiritual Care: The essence of chaplaincy is to provide spiritual care without judgment or fear of repercussions. Confidentiality allows chaplains to minister in a way that is free from the constraints of external scrutiny or institutional pressure.

2. Professional Codes of Conduct

Chaplains are often guided by professional codes of conduct that outline the ethical standards they must uphold, including confidentiality. Some of the widely recognized codes include:

The Association of Professional Chaplains (APC): The APC emphasizes the importance of confidentiality in its Code of Ethics, stating that chaplains must respect the privacy of individuals and ensure that information shared in confidence remains confidential unless there is a compelling reason to disclose it.

The National Association of Catholic Chaplains (NACC): The NACC's Code of Ethics highlights the importance of safeguarding the confidentiality of all communications, emphasizing the need for informed consent before sharing sensitive information.

The Spiritual Care Association (SCA): The SCA's ethical guidelines include the expectation that chaplains will maintain confidentiality in all professional relationships, reaffirming the trust that individuals place in them.

These codes provide a framework for chaplains to navigate ethical dilemmas and uphold their responsibility to maintain confidentiality.

Universal Ethical Dilemmas in Chaplaincy

Chaplains face universal ethical dilemmas that often arise from the sensitive nature of their work. These dilemmas require careful consideration and ethical reasoning. Some common dilemmas include:

Disclosure vs. Confidentiality: Chaplains may grapple with whether to disclose information that could protect someone from harm, weighing the risks of breaching confidentiality against the potential benefits of revealing critical information.

Autonomy vs. Beneficence: Chaplains may find themselves torn between respecting a patient's or inmate's autonomy and making decisions that are in their best interest. This dilemma arises when individuals refuse care or guidance that the chaplain believes is necessary for their well-being.

Cultural Sensitivity vs. Ethical Standards: In culturally diverse settings, chaplains may encounter practices or beliefs that challenge their ethical standards. Balancing cultural sensitivity while adhering to ethical principles can create ethical conflicts for chaplains.

Advocacy vs. Neutrality: Chaplains may struggle with the need to advocate for individuals while maintaining neutrality. This dilemma arises when chaplains must navigate their roles as spiritual caregivers while simultaneously representing the needs of those they serve.

Navigating Confidentiality in Prisons and Hospitals

Chaplains work in environments where sensitive information abounds, making it imperative to maintain confidentiality while navigating unique challenges inherent in prison and hospital settings.

1. Handling Sensitive Information

In both prisons and hospitals, chaplains encounter a wide range of sensitive information that requires careful handling. This includes:

Personal Histories: Inmates may share deeply personal stories related to their past, including trauma, addiction, and mental health struggles. Chaplains must approach these narratives with compassion while ensuring confidentiality is upheld.

Spiritual Struggles: Individuals often discuss their spiritual doubts, fears, and hopes during chaplaincy sessions. These discussions should remain confidential to foster a safe environment for exploration and healing.

Medical Conditions: In hospital settings, chaplains may receive information regarding patients' medical conditions and treatments. Respecting patient privacy is crucial, especially in environments where medical staff and family members may be present.

2. Practical Strategies for Maintaining Confidentiality

To navigate the challenges of confidentiality, chaplains can employ several practical strategies:

Create Private Spaces: Whenever possible, chaplains should conduct conversations in private settings to ensure confidentiality. In prisons, this may involve designated counseling rooms, while in hospitals, it may mean using quiet corners or private meeting areas.

Set Boundaries: Chaplains should establish clear boundaries regarding confidentiality at the outset of their interactions. They can explain to individuals the importance of confidentiality and the circumstances in which information may need to be shared.

Documenting Information: If chaplains must document sensitive information, they should ensure that it is stored securely and accessed only by authorized personnel. Maintaining separate records for personal spiritual care and institutional documentation can help protect privacy.

Use Caution in Group Settings: In group sessions, chaplains should remind participants of the importance of confidentiality and encourage them to respect each other's privacy. Facilitating discussions where participants share only what they are comfortable disclosing can help maintain trust.

Balancing Confidentiality and Advocacy

Chaplains often find themselves in advocacy roles, representing the interests of the individuals they serve. This can create tension between maintaining confidentiality and acting in the best interests of patients or prisoners.

1. Understanding the Role of Advocacy

Advocacy involves speaking on behalf of individuals, raising their concerns, and seeking to improve their circumstances. For chaplains, advocacy may take various forms:

Providing Support: Chaplains can advocate for individuals' emotional and spiritual needs by ensuring they receive appropriate care, access to programs, or connections with support services.

Facilitating Communication: Chaplains often act as intermediaries between individuals and institutional staff, helping communicate needs and concerns while respecting confidentiality.

Navigating Institutional Policies: In some cases, chaplains may advocate for policy changes within prisons or hospitals to better support the spiritual well-being of those they serve.

2. Protecting Sensitive Information While Advocating

While advocating for individuals, chaplains must protect sensitive information and maintain professional boundaries. This can be achieved through the following strategies:

Clarify Limits of Confidentiality: Before taking any advocacy steps, chaplains should clarify the limits of confidentiality with the individual involved. This ensures that individuals understand how their information may be used in the advocacy process.

Obtain Consent When Possible: When advocating on behalf of someone, chaplains should seek the individual's consent before sharing sensitive information. This promotes transparency and helps maintain trust.

Focus on Collective Concerns: When advocating for systemic changes or improvements, chaplains can focus on collective issues rather than individual cases. By raising broader concerns, they protect individual identities while still promoting the well-being of the community.

3. Navigating Ethical Dilemmas

Chaplains may face ethical dilemmas when balancing confidentiality and advocacy. In such situations, chaplains should consider the following:

Consult Ethical Guidelines: Referring to ethical guidelines and codes of conduct can help chaplains navigate complex situations and provide clarity on their responsibilities.

Seek Supervision or Guidance: Engaging in supervision or seeking guidance from colleagues can provide additional perspectives on challenging ethical dilemmas. Collaborative discussions can lead to informed decisions that respect confidentiality while advocating for the best interests of those served.

Conclusion

Confidentiality is a cornerstone of effective chaplaincy, serving as a foundation for trust and ethical practice. By understanding the ethical standards surrounding confidentiality, navigating sensitive information in prisons and hospitals, and balancing confidentiality with advocacy, chaplains can fulfill their calling with integrity and compassion.

In a world where vulnerability and suffering are prevalent, the ability to maintain confidentiality becomes an essential aspect of providing meaningful spiritual care. As chaplains strive to uphold confidentiality, they not only honor the individuals they serve but also strengthen the very fabric of their ministry, fostering healing and hope in the lives of those they encounter.

Being a chaplain requires a unique set of skills, a deep commitment to personal spiritual growth, and an understanding of the necessity for self-care. In this chapter, we will explore practical guidance on developing the skills needed for effective ministry, along with strategies for maintaining well-being and avoiding burnout. The emphasis is not only on serving others but also on nurturing oneself to ensure longevity and effectiveness in this vital vocation.

Developing Emotional Resilience

Chaplains are often immersed in emotionally charged situations, whether they are comforting a family facing a terminal illness, guiding inmates through the struggles of incarceration, or supporting healthcare staff amidst crises. Emotional resilience is key to sustaining their ministry and can be cultivated through various methods.

1. Emotional Detachment Techniques

Emotional detachment doesn't mean shutting down feelings; rather, it involves creating a healthy distance to maintain objectivity. Techniques to achieve this include:

Mindfulness Practices: Engaging in mindfulness can help chaplains observe their thoughts and feelings without becoming overwhelmed by them. Mindfulness practices, such as deep breathing and meditation, enable chaplains to ground themselves in the present moment, thereby managing their emotional responses.

Visualization: When entering emotionally intense environments, chaplains can visualize themselves as a conduit of support rather than the source of healing. This approach allows them to offer comfort without internalizing the pain of those they serve.

2. Reflective Practices

Regular reflection allows chaplains to process their experiences, recognize emotional triggers, and learn from their interactions. Effective reflective practices include:

Debriefing Sessions: Engaging in debriefing sessions with peers or supervisors can provide chaplains with an opportunity to discuss challenging experiences, share insights, and gather different perspectives on their ministry.

Supervision: Regular supervision from a more experienced chaplain or mental health professional can help chaplains gain clarity, guidance, and emotional support as they navigate complex situations.

3. Peer Support Networks

Building a network of support with other chaplains can be invaluable. Peer support networks allow chaplains to share experiences, provide encouragement, and discuss the challenges they face in a safe and confidential space. This shared camaraderie can alleviate feelings of isolation and reinforce emotional resilience.

Managing Stress and Avoiding Burnout

Chaplains often find themselves navigating the demanding emotional landscapes of those they serve. It is crucial to manage stress effectively and take proactive steps to avoid burnout. Here are some strategies:

1. Setting Boundaries

One of the most important skills for chaplains is establishing boundaries. These boundaries help maintain a healthy balance between personal life and ministry:

Work-Life Balance: Chaplains should designate specific times for work and personal activities, ensuring they allocate time for rest and rejuvenation outside of their ministry.

Emotional Boundaries: While it is important to empathize with those they serve, chaplains should guard against emotional overreach. By setting limits on how much emotional labor they invest in each interaction, they can maintain their well-being.

2. Personal Spiritual Renewal

Chaplains must prioritize their spiritual health to sustain their capacity to care for others. This can involve:

Engaging in Spiritual Practices: Regularly participating in spiritual practices, such as prayer, meditation, or worship, can nurture a chaplain's inner life and reconnect them with their calling.

Retreats: Attending spiritual retreats allows chaplains to step back from their daily responsibilities and engage in focused reflection, personal prayer, and renewal. These retreats provide a space for healing and reconnection with God.

3. Regular Self-Care Practices

Self-care is not a luxury; it is an essential component of effective ministry. Chaplains should incorporate self-care practices into their daily routines:

Physical Health: Maintaining physical health through exercise, nutrition, and adequate rest is crucial. Physical well-being can enhance emotional resilience and overall effectiveness in ministry.

Creative Outlets: Engaging in creative activities, such as art, music, or writing, can provide an emotional release and promote mental well-being.

Social Connections: Maintaining connections with family and friends outside of ministry can provide support and balance, helping chaplains recharge and gain perspective.

Reflective Practice: Journaling and Spiritual Direction

Reflective practice is a powerful tool for personal growth and spiritual development. It allows chaplains to process their experiences and nurture their inner lives while serving others.

1. Journaling

Journaling provides chaplains with an opportunity to articulate their thoughts and feelings, process experiences, and reflect on their spiritual journey. Benefits of journaling include:

Clarification of Thoughts: Writing down experiences can clarify emotions and thoughts, helping chaplains identify patterns and areas for growth.

Tracking Progress: Keeping a journal allows chaplains to track their spiritual and emotional progress over time, offering insights into their growth and challenges.

-

2. Spiritual Direction

Seeking spiritual direction involves meeting with a trained spiritual director who can guide chaplains in their spiritual journey. Spiritual direction offers:

Intentional Reflection: Spiritual directors provide a space for chaplains to reflect on their experiences, deepening their understanding of their call and purpose.

Accountability: Regular meetings with a spiritual director can hold chaplains accountable for their spiritual growth and self-care practices.

Continuing Education and Professional Development

The field of chaplaincy is constantly evolving, with new practices, theories, and insights emerging regularly. Chaplains must commit to ongoing education and professional development to stay current and effective in their ministry.

1. Pursuing Further Education

Chaplains can enhance their qualifications through formal education programs, including advanced degrees or specialized certifications in areas such as grief counseling, crisis intervention, or interfaith dialogue. Pursuing additional education can deepen their understanding of the complexities of spiritual care.

2. Attending Workshops and Conferences

Engaging in workshops, seminars, and conferences allows chaplains to learn from experienced professionals, explore new topics, and network with other chaplains. These experiences can offer fresh perspectives and innovative strategies for addressing the diverse needs of those they serve.

3. Engaging in Professional Networks

Joining professional organizations or networks for chaplains can provide ongoing support, resources, and opportunities for collaboration. Participation in these networks can foster a sense of community and encourage the sharing of best practices among chaplains.

Professional Ethical Codes of Chaplains

Chaplains are expected to adhere to a professional code of ethics that guides their practice and decision-making. These ethical codes serve as a framework for maintaining integrity, respect, and responsibility within their ministry. Key components of these codes often include:

1. Confidentiality

Chaplains must respect the confidentiality of those they serve, safeguarding sensitive information and trusting relationships. They must be aware of the boundaries of confidentiality and when it is appropriate to share information, particularly in cases of harm or legal requirements.

2. Respect for Diversity

Chaplains should honor and respect the diverse backgrounds, beliefs, and values of those they serve. This commitment to inclusivity fosters a safe and welcoming environment for individuals from various cultural and religious backgrounds.

3. Integrity and Honesty

Chaplains are expected to act with integrity and honesty in their interactions. This includes being truthful about their qualifications, capabilities, and the scope of their ministry.

4. Professional Competence

Chaplains should strive for continual professional development and education, ensuring they remain competent in their roles. This includes staying informed about current trends and best practices in spiritual care.

5. Advocacy

Chaplains have a responsibility to advocate for the spiritual and emotional well-being of those they serve. This may involve speaking up for individuals' rights and needs within institutional settings, whether in prisons, hospitals, or other environments.

6. Self-Care

Chaplains are encouraged to prioritize their self-care, recognizing that their well-being directly impacts their ability to serve effectively. They should seek support and resources to maintain their mental, emotional, and spiritual health.

7. Accountability

Chaplains should hold themselves accountable for their actions and decisions, recognizing their role as spiritual leaders. They should seek feedback and supervision to enhance their practice and ensure they meet ethical standards.

Conclusion

In conclusion, effective chaplaincy requires a unique blend of practical skills, emotional resilience, and a commitment to self-care. As chaplains navigate the complexities of their ministry, it is essential to develop emotional resilience, manage stress, engage in reflective practices, and pursue continuing education. By adhering to a professional ethical code, chaplains can maintain integrity and responsibility in their work. By prioritizing their own spiritual and emotional well-being, chaplains can sustain their ability to serve others compassionately and effectively, fostering healing and hope in the lives of those they encounter.

Building a sustainable and effective chaplaincy ministry is both a challenging and rewarding endeavor. It requires collaboration, careful planning, and a clear vision for the future. This chapter outlines practical steps to establish and grow a chaplaincy program in prisons, hospitals, and other institutions, highlighting key areas of focus such as collaboration, program establishment, fundraising, and mentoring future chaplains.

Collaborating with Churches and Religious Communities

Chaplains do not operate in a vacuum; their effectiveness is often enhanced by building strong relationships with local churches, religious communities, and service organizations. Collaboration with these entities can lead to a more robust ministry that meets the diverse needs of those being served.

1. Building Partnerships

Creating meaningful partnerships with local churches and religious organizations is essential for sustaining chaplaincy work. Here are several strategies for building these relationships:

Outreach Programs: Establish outreach initiatives that connect churches with chaplaincy work. This could include hosting informational meetings, workshops, or community events that educate congregations about the role of chaplains in hospitals and prisons. By showcasing the impact of chaplaincy, you can inspire congregations to become actively involved.

Volunteer Engagement: Encourage churches to mobilize volunteers who can support chaplaincy initiatives. Volunteers can assist in various ways, from providing administrative support to participating in spiritual care activities. Engaging church members creates a sense of ownership and community involvement in the chaplaincy program.

Shared Resources: Collaborate with churches to share resources, such as meeting spaces, funding for events, or materials for outreach. Building resource-sharing agreements can strengthen relationships and enhance the capabilities of both chaplains and congregations.

2. Fundraising Collaboration

Engaging local religious communities in fundraising efforts can significantly bolster chaplaincy programs. Churches can host special offerings, fundraising events, or campaigns that specifically support chaplaincy initiatives. Collaborative fundraising helps raise awareness about the ministry's needs and inspires congregations to contribute financially.

Establishing Chaplaincy Programs in Prisons and Hospitals

Starting a chaplaincy program from the ground up involves careful planning and securing institutional support. Here are practical steps to follow:

1. Assessing Needs

Conduct a needs assessment to understand the specific spiritual care requirements of the target population. This assessment should involve conversations with prison administrators, hospital staff, and potential chaplaincy clients. Understanding the unique challenges and needs of those you will serve will inform the program's design.

2. Gaining Institutional Backing

Securing institutional backing is crucial for establishing a chaplaincy program. Here's how to approach this task:

Develop a Proposal: Craft a comprehensive proposal outlining the goals, objectives, and expected outcomes of the chaplaincy program. Highlight the benefits to the institution, such as improved mental health outcomes, enhanced inmate rehabilitation, or increased patient satisfaction.

Present to Key Stakeholders: Identify key decision-makers within the institution, such as hospital administrators or prison wardens, and present your proposal. Highlight how spiritual care aligns with the institution's mission and vision, emphasizing the importance of holistic care for those in their care.

3. Building a Team

A successful chaplaincy program requires a dedicated team of chaplains and volunteers. Here are some strategies for assembling this team:

Recruitment: Identify and recruit qualified individuals who have a passion for chaplaincy work. This could include experienced chaplains, seminary students, or volunteers from local churches. Clearly define roles and responsibilities to ensure a well-functioning team.

Training and Orientation: Provide thorough training and orientation for all team members. This should cover essential topics such as ethics, communication skills, and the specific needs of the population being served. Building a cohesive team will enhance the overall effectiveness of the ministry.

Fundraising and Securing Support

Funding is often a significant challenge for chaplaincy programs, particularly those that operate independently of religious institutions. Here are strategies for securing financial support:

1. Grant Proposals

Writing grant proposals can be a valuable way to secure funding for chaplaincy initiatives. Consider the following steps:

Research Grant Opportunities: Identify potential grant opportunities from foundations, government agencies, and nonprofit organizations that support health, justice, and spiritual care initiatives.

Tailor Proposals: Tailor your grant proposals to align with the specific goals and priorities of the funding organization. Clearly articulate the impact of your chaplaincy program on the community and the populations served.

2. Church Support

Engaging local churches and religious communities for financial support is crucial. Strategies include:

Regular Appeals: Make regular appeals to local congregations, sharing stories of impact and need. Use newsletters, church bulletins, and presentations to highlight the importance of chaplaincy work and encourage giving.

Special Events: Organize special fundraising events in collaboration with churches, such as charity dinners, auctions, or community service projects. These events can raise awareness and funds for chaplaincy initiatives while strengthening relationships with congregations.

3. Community Engagement

Explore partnerships with local nonprofits and community organizations that may share similar goals. These partnerships can provide financial support, in-kind donations, or collaborative programming opportunities that enhance the chaplaincy ministry.

Mentoring and Training Future Chaplains

Building a sustainable ministry includes ensuring that future chaplains are trained, mentored, and equipped for the challenges of their vocation. Here are ways to develop future leaders in chaplaincy:

1. Mentorship Programs

Establish mentorship programs that connect experienced chaplains with those in training or new to the field. These mentorship relationships can provide guidance, support, and wisdom as individuals navigate the complexities of chaplaincy.

- **Structured Mentorship**: Create a structured mentorship program that includes regular meetings, goal-setting, and evaluation. This will ensure that mentees receive the support and guidance they need to develop their skills and confidence.

2. Training Opportunities

Offer training opportunities to equip future chaplains with the necessary skills and knowledge. Consider:

Workshops and Seminars: Organize workshops on topics such as grief counseling, crisis intervention, and interfaith dialogue. These trainings can be tailored to meet the specific needs of the chaplains being trained.

Field Experience: Provide opportunities for chaplain candidates to gain practical experience through internships or clinical pastoral education (CPE) programs. Hands-on experience is invaluable for developing competence and confidence in their roles.

3. Creating a Pipeline of New Chaplains

To ensure the ongoing growth and sustainability of chaplaincy programs, consider creating a pipeline for new chaplains:

Partnerships with Seminaries: Collaborate with theological schools and seminaries to offer internships and placements for students pursuing chaplaincy. This partnership can create a steady flow of trained individuals into the ministry.

Continuing Education: Encourage ongoing education and professional development for both current and future chaplains, ensuring they stay informed and competent in their field.

Conclusion

Building a sustainable and effective chaplaincy ministry is a multifaceted endeavor that requires collaboration, careful planning, and an unwavering commitment to the spiritual and emotional well-being of those served. By establishing strong partnerships with churches and religious communities, creating impactful chaplaincy programs, securing funding, and mentoring future chaplains, chaplains can foster a thriving ministry that meets the diverse needs of individuals in prisons, hospitals, and beyond. Through this dedicated effort, chaplains not only fulfill their calling but also bring hope and healing to the lives of countless individuals.

CHAPTER 10
The Hope of Tomorrow: A Vision for Chaplaincy

The ministry of chaplaincy offers profound hope in a broken world. It is a calling that transcends the ordinary, inviting individuals to enter into the sacred space of another's life during their most vulnerable moments. As we conclude this exploration of chaplaincy, it is essential to reflect on the future of this ministry, envisioning a landscape where hope, restoration, and healing flourish.

The Future of Chaplaincy in a Changing World

As society evolves, so too must the practice of chaplaincy. Emerging trends shape the landscape of spiritual care, revealing both challenges and opportunities for chaplains. The growing need for interfaith ministry highlights the importance of inclusivity, as people from diverse backgrounds seek spiritual guidance in settings where traditional religious affiliations may no longer suffice. Chaplains must cultivate an understanding of various belief systems while remaining grounded in their own faith, becoming bridges that foster connection rather than division.

Technology is also reshaping the way spiritual care is delivered. Virtual counseling sessions, online support groups, and digital resources enable chaplains to reach individuals who may otherwise feel isolated. As the world becomes more interconnected through technology, chaplains must embrace these tools while ensuring that the essence of compassionate, personal connection remains central to their ministry.

Moreover, chaplains face the ongoing challenge of ministering in an increasingly secular world. The decline of traditional religious practices and the rise of skepticism can create barriers for chaplains seeking to engage with individuals. However, this shift also presents an opportunity for chaplains to articulate the universal themes of love, compassion, and hope—principles that resonate deeply, regardless of one's spiritual beliefs. In this way, chaplains can invite individuals to explore their own spirituality, even in the absence of formal religious frameworks.

Answering the Call: Encouragement for Future Chaplains

For those considering the call to chaplaincy, it is essential to acknowledge both the challenges and the rewards of this vocation. It is not an easy path; the emotional toll of walking alongside individuals in crisis can weigh heavily. Yet, it is precisely in these moments of suffering that chaplains have the unique opportunity to be vessels of God's love and grace.

To those feeling a stirring in their hearts toward chaplaincy, embrace your calling with courage. Understand that your presence can bring hope to the hopeless, comfort to the grieving, and healing to the broken. Remember the words of the Apostle Paul: "And we know that in all things God works for the good of those who love him, who have been called according to his purpose" (Romans 8:28). Your work as a chaplain is part of this divine purpose, an invitation to participate in God's redemptive work in the world.

As you embark on this journey, remain steadfast in your faith. Engage in prayer, seek mentorship, and continue your education. Surround yourself with a community of support—fellow chaplains, spiritual leaders, and friends who understand the complexities of this calling. Know that you are not alone; God walks with you, equipping you with everything you need to fulfill your mission.

Conclusion

In conclusion, *The Call to Chaplaincy: A Practical Guide to Prison and Hospital Ministry* is an invitation to a sacred and challenging vocation. Chaplaincy is a ministry of presence, healing, and hope. Whether in prisons, hospitals, or other settings, chaplains are called to walk alongside those who suffer, offering spiritual guidance, emotional support, and the hope of transformation.

As you continue your journey in chaplaincy, may this guide serve as a companion, providing encouragement, practical tools, and spiritual nourishment as you answer the call to serve. Remember that in your ministry, you carry the light of hope into the darkest corners of the human experience, helping others to discover the profound promise of tomorrow—a promise rooted in love, grace, and the possibility of renewal.

Appendix: Code of Conduct for Chaplains

As representatives of spiritual care and guidance, chaplains are called to uphold a high standard of ethical behavior that reflects the teachings of Christ, the Pauline Gospel, and relevant philosophical principles. This code of conduct serves as a guiding framework for chaplains in their ministry, emphasizing the importance of integrity, compassion, and service.

1. Commitment to Service

Chaplains shall dedicate themselves to serving others selflessly, following the example of Christ, who said, "For even the Son of Man did not come to be served, but to serve" (Mark 10:45). This commitment includes:

- **Selflessness**: Placing the needs of others before personal interests.
- **Accessibility**: Being available and approachable to those in need, demonstrating a willingness to listen and provide care.

2. Respect for Dignity

Recognizing the inherent dignity of every individual is essential in chaplaincy. In accordance with the Pauline teaching of "bearing one another's burdens" (Galatians 6:2), chaplains shall:

- **Honor Diversity**: Respect the diverse beliefs, cultures, and backgrounds of individuals, providing care that is inclusive and sensitive.
- **Foster Respect**: Create a safe environment where individuals feel valued and heard, regardless of their circumstances.

3. Confidentiality and Trust

Maintaining confidentiality is a sacred responsibility rooted in the trust placed in chaplains by those they serve. Chaplains shall:

- **Protect Privacy**: Safeguard personal information and spiritual concerns shared by individuals, only disclosing information when legally mandated or when there is a risk of harm.
- **Build Trust**: Establish and maintain trusting relationships by being honest, transparent, and consistent in their actions.

4. Spiritual Integrity

Chaplains are called to embody and promote spiritual integrity, reflecting the teachings of Christ and the wisdom of the Apostle Paul. This includes:

- **Authenticity**: Living in alignment with one's spiritual beliefs and values, demonstrating honesty in words and actions.
- **Humility**: Approaching ministry with humility, recognizing that spiritual growth is a continuous journey, both for the chaplain and those served.

5. Compassionate Care

Compassion is at the heart of chaplaincy. Following Christ's example of love and care for others, chaplains shall:

- **Practice Empathy**: Strive to understand and share in the feelings and experiences of those they serve, offering support and validation.
- **Provide Hope**: Share messages of hope, healing, and redemption, encouraging individuals to seek a deeper connection with the Divine.

6. Ethical Decision-Making

In situations where ethical dilemmas arise, chaplains are called to navigate these challenges with integrity and discernment, guided by the principles of love and justice found in the Scriptures. Chaplains shall:

- **Seek Wisdom**: Engage in prayerful reflection and consult with colleagues and mentors when faced with difficult ethical decisions.
- **Act Justly**: Uphold justice, fairness, and equity in their interactions with individuals, advocating for those who may be marginalized or oppressed.

7. Professional Development

Chaplains shall commit to ongoing personal and professional growth to enhance their effectiveness in ministry. This includes:

- **Continuing Education**: Actively seek opportunities for education, training, and professional development, staying informed about best practices in spiritual care.
- **Reflective Practice**: Engage in regular reflection, self-assessment, and supervision to identify areas for growth and improvement.

8. Collaboration and Community Engagement

Chaplains are called to work collaboratively with others, recognizing the value of community in the healing process. They shall:

- **Foster Collaboration**: Work alongside healthcare professionals, correctional staff, and community organizations to provide holistic care that addresses the spiritual, emotional, and physical needs of individuals.
- **Engage the Community**: Participate in community initiatives that promote healing and well-being, serving as a bridge between the institutional setting and the wider community.

This Code of Conduct serves as a guiding framework for chaplains, reflecting the teachings of Christ, the wisdom of the Pauline Gospel, and the philosophical underpinnings of ethical conduct. By embodying these principles, chaplains can fulfill their calling to provide compassionate, respectful, and effective spiritual care to those they serve

Don't miss out!

Visit the website below and you can sign up to receive emails whenever Kayumba David publishes a new book. There's no charge and no obligation.

https://books2read.com/r/B-A-KRSOC-AXRHF

BOOKS2READ

Connecting independent readers to independent writers.

Did you love *Hope and Recovery - A Chaplain's Handbook*? Then you should read *Thanks to Calvary: A Salvific Treatise on the Cross*[1] by Kayumba David!

The cross of Jesus Christ is the axis of human history, the event upon which the fate of all creation hinges. This book, *"Thanks to Calvary: A Salvific Treatise on the Cross"*, represents years of contemplation, prayer, and engagement with the profound truths revealed in Scripture. As I delved into the Pauline understanding of the cross, I realized that it offers more than just theological insight; it provides the assurance of salvation, the end of religious striving, and the dawn of grace.

Growing up, I often grappled with questions about salvation, guilt, and whether I was truly "right" with God. It was the teaching of the Apostle Paul, especially his exposition of the cross, that opened my

---

1. https://books2read.com/u/4XADX9

2. https://books2read.com/u/4XADX9

eyes to the finality of Christ's work. I discovered that Calvary was not merely an event to be remembered; it was a reality to be experienced. The cross, as Dr. Desmond Ford once said, is "God's final word on sin and grace" (Ford, *The Cross and Grace*, p. 3). In it, I found hope, freedom, and certainty. Throughout this work, I draw from esteemed scholars and theologians, including Dr. Ford, Charles Spurgeon, and Hauwar Stanely. These men have illuminated the depths of Pauline theology and the centrality of the cross in ways that continue to inspire and convict me. Their writings have enriched my understanding and compelled me to share these truths with a wider audience.

This book aims to articulate the all-encompassing significance of the cross of Jesus Christ. It is my prayer that as you journey through these pages, you will see the cross not merely as a religious symbol, but as the transformative event that forever changed the cosmos, conquered sin, and offers the assurance of salvation for all who believe. In a world where religious uncertainty often clouds faith, may the message of Calvary shine brightly as a beacon of hope.

Thank you for joining me on this journey. To God alone be the glory.

Kayumba David

Read more at www.zcews.org.

About the Author

Kayumba David is an accomplished author known for his works that span across themes of spirituality, African experiences, and healthcare chaplaincy. His writings often delve into profound social, political, and personal subjects.

One of his notable works is "Visas: The Irony of Freedom", where he critiques the paradoxes faced by many Africans regarding international travel and freedom

He also authored "Hope and Healing: A Chaplain's Handbook," which reflects on his experiences as a chaplain and emphasizes the importance of compassion and spiritual care in healthcare and prison environments

Kayumba's works reflect his personal journey through theological study and lay ministry, having faced challenges within religious institutions, especially during his time in Belgium, where he became an advocate for open theological debate

His contributions in literature offer insights into African realities, the complexities of modern spirituality, and the role of chaplaincy in emotional healing.

Read more at www.zcews.org.